India Stinking:
Manual scavengers in Andhra Pradesh and their work

Forthcoming from Navayana

The Blindness of Insight: Why Communalism is about Caste and other essays. By Dilip Menon

Namdeo: Poet of the Underworld; The Life, Work and Times of Namdeo Dhasal. By Dilip Chitre

Kilvenmani, 25 December 1968. By Stalin Rajangam

Karamchedu, Chunduru and Beyond: Dalit Movement in Andhra Pradesh. By K. Srinivasulu

Meenakshipuram, 1981: Understanding Mass Conversion of Dalits to Islam. By M.A. Kalam

Other titles

Dalits in Dravidian Land: Frontline Reports on Anti-Dalit Violence in Tamil Nadu (1995–2004).
By S. Viswanathan   ISBN 81-89059-05-X

Dalit Diary: 1999-2003. Reflections on Apartheid in India.
By Chandra Bhan Prasad   ISBN 81-89059-04-1

Touchable Tales: Publishing and Reading Dalit Literature.
Ed. S. Anand   ISBN 81-89059-00-9

Ambedkar: Autobiographical Notes.
By B.R. Ambedkar   ISBN 81-89059-01-7

*Postmodernism and Religious Fundamentalism:
A Scientific Rebuttal to Hindu Science.*
By Meera Nanda   ISBN 81-89059-02-5

Brahmans and Cricket: Lagaan's Millennial Purana and Other Myths
By S. Anand   ISBN 81-89059-03-3

India Stinking:
Manual scavengers in Andhra Pradesh and their work

Gita Ramaswamy

India Stinking:
Manual scavengers in Andhra Pradesh and their work

© Navayana Publishing, 2005

ISBN 81-89059-06-8

The proceeds from the sale of this book will go towards ensuring that the children of M. Jayaraman, Kanniamma and N. Poliah (sanitation workers of IV Seaward Road, Valmiki Nagar, Thiruvanmiyur, Chennai 600041) are liberated from this profession and settled in alternative livelihoods. For details, contact Shiva Shankar sshankar@cmi.ac.in

No part of this book may be reproduced or utilised in any form without the prior permission of the publisher.

Cover and book design by DESIGN WORKS

Typeset in CG Omega
by Trinity Designers and Typesetters, Chennai

Printed by Quadra Press, Chennai

Published by Ravikumar and S. Anand for Navayana Publishing

Registered Office
54, I Floor, Savarirayalu Street
Pondicherry 605008
www.navayana.org, navayana@navayana.org, navayana@ambedkar.org
91-9444061256, 91-9345419266

Distributed by IPD Alternatives, New Delhi
and WestLand Books Pvt. Ltd., Chennai

Stockist
Oasis Books, 17 Kutchery Road
Mylapore, Chennai 600004
91-44-24613445

Contents

Foreword   vi
Preface   x
1. Manual Scavenging   1
2. Who are the Scavengers?   3
3. Practice and Prevalence: A Historical Overview   5
4. Scavenging and Caste   14
5. What has been Done to Stop Scavenging?   21
6. How Widespread is Manual Scavenging Today?   30
7. Bezwada Wilson: Shepherd of the Manual Scavengers   41
8. Safai Karamchari Andolan   49
9. The Struggle for Self-Respect   54
10. A Community in Transition   65
11. What You Can Do   68
Appendix 1: Organisations to help initiate action against manual scavenging   71
Appendix 2: Employment of Manual Scavengers and Construction of Dry Latrines (Prohibition) Act, 1993   73
Appendix 3: District-wise breakup of community dry latrines in Andhra Pradesh   84
Appendix 4: Mohandas Gandhi on Scavenging   86
Appendix 5: B.R. Ambedkar on Scavenging   96
Select Bibliography   107

Foreword

Manual scavenging rests on the foundation of the caste system. Manual scavenging is the worst expression of the beliefs engendered by the caste system—untouchability, purity–pollution, dharma and karma. Caste Hindus may disagree and argue that the practice of manual scavenging is only an aberration of the caste system; that it is one of the problems in the system that need to be fixed. I have come to realise that the elimination of manual scavenging is not possible without rocking the boat of caste hierarchy; and the caste Hindus are afraid of doing that. How else can I understand the presence of a dry toilet in the municipal court in Nizamabad and the written order prohibiting the Safai Karamchari Andolan from even symbolically demolishing it? It is not only a painful symbol of our past but also of our present. Let the future not inherit this.

The Government of India promulgated 'The Employment of Manual Scavengers and Construction of Dry Latrines (Prohibition) Act' in 1993. However, to this day an estimated 13,00,000 people[1] from dalit communities continue to be employed as manual scavengers across the length and breadth of this country—in private homes, in community dry latrines (CDLs) managed by the municipality, in the public sector such as railways, and by the army. In Andhra Pradesh, there are 8,330 manual scavengers employed in over 1,600 CDLs and over 1.5 lakh individual dry latrines.

For a country of our size and resources, eliminating this practice and rehabilitating the safai karamcharis is not an impossible task. The government has invested in different committees, commissions and missions to examine the various aspects of the problem. Funds are allocated for educating civil society on health and sanitation. Subsidies are offered for the construction of pour-flush toilets. However, not a single person has been charged with or prosecuted for employing manual scavengers despite the Act. Twelve years after the belated ban, neither the state nor civil society has faith in our intentions.

The state has been more than indifferent about what it initiated. The Act was made in 1993 but it was not notified in the Gazette of India till 1997. No state promulgated the Act till 2000. How do we understand the ministry of railways saying that the cost factor has to be considered if they have to eliminate the practice? How do we understand the municipalities that continue to construct and employ safai karamcharis to clean the dry toilets? How do we understand a court issuing a written order that the dry toilet on its premises cannot be demolished because it is government property? How do we understand the many individuals in this society who complain that the safai karamcharis have not done a clean job despite being paid to do so? It is not the lack of technology, not the lack of budgets, nor is it the absence or existence of a legal framework that stands in the way of the abolition of this practice: it is our caste mindset built on the base of social exclusion and economic exploitation.

I am the son of manual scavengers who worked for two generations to extract gold in the Kolar Gold Fields, Karnakata. I lay down near the shit-dumping pit and wept my heart out when I was old enough to understand the plight of my people. I fail to understand Gandhiji, who glorified the task of the manual scavengers comparing it to the service of a mother to her children. How can one feel proud of cleaning the worm-filled, stench-producing shits of millions every day? Instinctively closing our nostrils, filling our chests with what fresh air we can muster before entering these toilets, we safai karamcharis suffer from the worst kinds of respiratory and skin infections. Like Narayanamma from Anantapur—featured on the cover of this book—many would tell us how at the age of eight or eleven they were introduced to this work; how for many days they could not bring food to their lips; how the stench of shit was constantly in their nostrils; how their intestines retched; how they were constantly spitting out the shame and the indignity. It is a sadder fact that the majority of manual scavengers are women.

The pity is also that we safai karamcharis did not accept Babasaheb Ambedkar as our leader when he thundered that this occupation should not be glorified but banned with immediate effect. Divided within ourselves, we did not use the momentum of the rest of the dalit movements to further our cause.

Working on this issue for two decades, and having organised the Safai Karamchari Andolan over the past decade, I am convinced that manual scavenging will not be eliminated and safai karamcharis will not be liberated as long as we, the Indian civil society, are not liberated from our caste mindset.

Very often nondalits and dalits—even safai karamcharis—question me: 'What alternatives do we have? How will they survive if they do not have even this occupation?' I can say with conviction that it is not concerns about livelihood that cause these doubts; it is the caste mindset and caste values. As a citizen of this country, with a legacy of great civilisations, my demand is that we liberate ourselves from this mindset; my brothers and sisters would be automatically liberated. We invite more friends to take up the issue and join us in this struggle for liberation.

I would like to thank Gita Ramaswamy for taking the effort to write this book. It places the issues squarely from the perspective of the community members. I am happy that the book also describes, in brief, the evolution and the work of the Safai Karamchari Andolan. The SKA is a movement that has its roots in the youth of the community whose sole aim is the elimination of manual scavenging and the liberation of safai karamcharis. The SKA has been strengthened and supported by the active involvement of a few individuals who were able to discard values instilled by the caste mindset. In particular, I must mention S.R. Sankaran, who has been vitally connected with the SKA, an organic linkage I am proud to acknowledge.

Bezwada Wilson
July 2005

---

1   The official estimate of the Ministry of Social Justice and Empowerment, Government of India, for 2002–03 is 6.76 lakh manual scavengers.

Preface

This book is an effort to bring to light the hidden practice of manual scavenging in Andhra Pradesh. Articles have appeared in newspapers and magazines; the issue stays in focus for a few days and then disappears from the public eye. A book, however, remains to disturb public consciousness for a longer period.

We need to ask ourselves why, in 2005, shit in thousands of latrines, both community and individual, needs to be manually removed. Working with the Safai Karamchari Andolan, I have tried to understand the issue through the lens of the caste system, which I feel has been largely responsible for this practice. This book seeks to understand, through the daily lives of the scavengers, what forces them to continue in this occupation. It also tries to chart the rise and growth of the Safai Karamchari Andolan (SKA), and the agency it has roused among scavengers.

While several people have given me generously of their time and valuable insights, S. R. Sankaran, a retired bureaucrat who has worked to bend the administration to the needs of the dalits, and Bezwada Wilson, leader of the Safai Karamchari Andolan in Andhra Pradesh, shared the burden of educating me. The scavengers of Chirala and Nandikotkur, and all those I met at the 16 September 2004 meeting in Hyderabad (where SKA's demolition drive culminated), were so open about their work, its nature, and its effects on them, that I stand humbled. I am thankful to the SKA and its members for allowing me to explore freely. I am not of the community, and am not privy to the insights that long years of participation and observation bring to a problem. The book therefore suffers from these limitations. It was written originally for a Telugu audience to bring home the facts of manual scavenging in Andhra Pradesh. Vimala, co-author of the book in Telugu (*Maakkoddee Chandalam*, Hyderabad Book Trust, 2005), contributed to the Telugu version, helped me conduct several field interviews, and has been an integral part of the English book too through her frequent interventions. The understanding of scavenging in Hyderabad, and the interactions with the methars, entirely owe to her. The book has been substantially revised for this English edition. I thank the University of Southampton for facilitating a study of the manual scavengers of Andhra Pradesh, on which this book is based.

It would be useful, and perhaps necessary, to explain my interest and involvement with the SKA. I had been associated with dry toilet scavengers earlier. After quitting the radical Left (Communist Party of India–Marxist-Leninist) in Andhra Pradesh in late 1975, my husband Cyril Reddy and I stayed and worked with the bhangis near Ghaziabad for a little more than two years (1978–80). We had felt the need to get away from party-driven ideology and work with people on their own felt needs. I do not know why we chanced on the bhangis to work with, but we initially visited them and asked them what we, an educated south Indian couple, could do with them. They asked us to tutor their children in studies, teach adult males English and the women sewing. We took up a room there and began work. I would watch the women return every day at noon with head-loads of shit that they would empty in the open field in front of their colony. The men worked as permanent workers in the railways and other establishments, doing similar work. It shames me now to write that apart from worrying whether I would get tapeworms from the pork I ate daily in their houses (the pigs fed off the shit that was dumped in the field), I did not think twice about their work and its nature. In classic Left style, I worried over the low wages they were making, not the nature of the work itself.

I recall that I prepared a Hindi primer that helped them to read and write in a month. The primer was based on the story of a woman safai karamchari, and I drew pictures of the woman, her work and her environment for each lesson. I accompanied them to various places—weddings, relatives' houses and the cinema, where I met hundreds of other people who did similar work. During this entire period, there was the singular absence of any reflection on my part on why they had to be doing this work at all. After a major stint in publishing, I reverted to work with dalits between 1984–91, and participated actively in the Dalit Mahasabha movements of that time. Despite this, it shakes me now to admit that if I had not heard of the SKA and its work, I would not have opened my eyes to the issue of why some people clean shit and why the rest of us do not worry our heads over this.

When I first heard of the SKA in 2001, I felt the issue was important. As I was primarily a publisher in Telugu, I had wanted a book to be published in Telugu about manual scavenging. Wilson and I met and discussed this on a few occasions; the understanding was that Wilson himself would write it. Nothing came of it. In 2004, the SKA invited me to participate in their statewide demolition drive. As a publisher, my participation would have been symbolic (of the token participation of notables) if it were not for the fact that the SKA visited Ibrahimpatnam, 30 km from Hyderabad, where I had worked with dalits between 1984–91. There they discovered that sixty-year-old Subiri of the methar community was cleaning twenty Individual Dry Latrines (IDLS) every day. This was a matter of great personal shame for me; I realised that I was like every other privileged caste Hindu in society—complicit in getting manual scavengers to clean shit by simply being 'unaware' of it. It was then that I decided that the book had to be done here and now since it was unlikely that anyone in the SKA, given the activist nature of their work, would do it.

1
Manual Scavenging

Sitting down to eat each night, my thoughts would go back to my day's work and I could not swallow a morsel. I even stopped this work for some time. But what could I do? My husband did nothing to look after the family and we were always short of food.
— Kamala, Hyderabad

We soil ourselves, so that others can look clean.
— Kotamma, Chirala

Manual scavenging in India is the lifting and removal of human excreta manually, both at private homes and in toilets maintained by public authorities. Manual scavenging is done in either of two ways. First, it is through dry toilets, where human excreta is left on a stone, plate, mud, or in a bucket. The manual scavenger must take the excreta to a place of disposal. Second, manual scavengers clean sewage pits, both in private homes and in municipalities. While private pits are cleaned under cover of darkness, it is a common sight to find men opening manholes to go down and manually clean sewers.

Manual scavenging was banned by a formal Act of parliament in 1993. It is called the Employment of Manual Scavengers and Construction of Dry Latrines (Prohibition) Act. Using or maintaining dry toilets is illegal and liable for criminal punishment, along with a fine. However, official statistics released by the Ministry of Social

Justice and Empowerment, Government of India, for 2002–03, reveal that there are 6.76 lakh manual scavengers in the country, spread over twenty-one states and union territories, working at 96 lakh dry latrines.[1] In Andhra Pradesh alone, there are between two and three lakh dry latrines, and local authorities actively maintain and support them.[2]

This tract provides a historical overview of manual scavenging; identifies the issues related to it; and reports the efforts made to combat the practice, especially the work of Bezwada Wilson, and the rise of the people's movement led by him—Safai Karamchari Andolan.

---

1 Figures quoted in the sworn affidavit of the SKA before the Supreme Court, 2003. A public interest petition was filed by the SKA and six other associate organisations and seven individual manual scavengers in the Supreme Court in 2003. The Supreme Court had agreed "that the number of manual scavengers has increased from 5.88 lakhs in 1992 to 7.87 lakhs." The unofficial count is estimated at 12 lakhs. (See "A Case for Human Dignity," *Frontline*, 17 June 2005).

2 Individual dry latrines are not completely enumerated in Andhra Pradesh. Hence the SKA has estimated that the number of IDLs is of this order. See p. 30–31.

2

Who are the Scavengers?

They go by many names in various parts of the country: han, hadi (in Bengal); balmiki, dhanuk (Uttar Pradesh); methar, bhangi (Assam); methar (Hyderabad); paki (coastal Andhra Pradesh); thotti (Tamil Nadu); mira, lalbegi, chuhra, balashahi (Punjab); bhangi, balmiki, methar, chuhra (Delhi).

Whatever they are called, they belong to the bottom of the Hindu social hierarchy: they are untouchables. Indeed, manual scavenging and untouchability—caste discrimination—go together. Castes that consider themselves superior enjoy a wider range of choice of occupations compared to other castes. The dalits, traditionally, have the least desirable occupations—cleaning, sweeping, leatherwork, removal of human excreta, removal of human and cattle corpses, rearing of scavenger pigs and suchlike. While there are many castes among the dalits, scavenging is the occupation of a few among them.

The elderly in the methar community (migrant balmikis from north India) in the Metharwadi settlement in Sultan Shahi municipal ward of the Old City of Hyderabad assert that they had not historically handled human faeces. "We removed dead animals, skinned cows, announced the death of people in the village, cleaned and removed animal dung (although this honour is not allowed to balmikis in many parts of India and Nepal, where animals, especially cows and therefore their sheds are considered [more] sacred than this group of humans). We were usually not allowed within the habitations of the upper castes and there was widespread open-field defecation."[1]

Methars (also sometimes spelt mehtars)[2] were brought from Haryana by Nizam-ul-Mulk Asaf Jah's government between 1855–60 to clean Telangana's shit; the Rayalaseema area brought in madigas from Nellore; in north Andhra, East Godavari, West Godavari and Krishna districts, rellis (a subcaste of the madigas) were employed; in Ongole and Guntur and a part of Nellore, yanadis were used; and in the Karnataka-bordering areas of Anantapur, halalkhors (a Muslim sect)[3] were used.[4] Those who scavenge for a living are not really set apart from the rest of the dalits.[5] Among the scavengers themselves, both men and women work, though women do the more regular, arduous tasks.

---

1 Deepa Joshi, "Gender, Urban Sanitation and Livelihoods," (*forthcoming*, Southampton: University of Southampton Press).
2 Methar literally means a prince or leader. Even today leaders of several caste panchayats in Andhra Pradesh are called methars.
3 Halalkhor is one who eats what is unlawful, or one whose earnings are not legitimate.
4 Vijay Prashad, in his seminal work *Untouchable Freedom: A Social History of a Dalit Community* (New Delhi: OUP, 2000) describes how the chuhris were brought in from Punjab for cleaning work in Delhi.
5 In their respective areas, both scavenging and non-scavenging castes intermingle and interdine. Intermarriage is less common.

3

Practice and Prevalence: A Historical Overview

Manual scavenging is prevalent across Asia. Migrants from Andhra Pradesh went to Bangladesh and Sri Lanka to do this work.[1] Other references to manual scavenging indicate that bucket toilets were prevalent in Africa and the Far East; China had manual scavengers (though they were not members of any caste).[2] Vault toilets (emptied by vacuum trucks) are still operable in Japan.

Manual scavenging in India has had a mixed lineage. Excavations in Lothal (62 km from Ahmedabad) show that in the Harappan civilisation in 2500 BCE, people had waterborne toilets in each house, which were linked by drains covered by burnt clay bricks. To facilitate operations and maintenance, this drainage system had manholes and chambers. But with the decline of the Indus Valley civilisation, the science of sanitary engineering suffered a setback. In a later period, we find that one of the fifteen duties for slaves enumerated in the *Narada Samhita* was the disposal of human excreta. In *Vajasaneyi Samhita*, chandalas were referred to as slaves engaged in the disposal of human excreta.[3]

Amit Mitra, an editor with the magazine *Down to Earth*, researched India's sophisticated sewage systems in medieval times. Bathing rooms of the Mughal forts had small outlets for excretion. Gravity carried the waste down and out to the ramparts with the water. This can be found in the Red Fort in Delhi, in the palaces of Rajasthan, in Hampi in Karnataka, and in Thiruvananthapuram, Kerala.[4]

Some controversy surrounds the Mughal period. A few argue that scavenging came in with the Mughals.[5] Prisoners of war were forced into manual scavenging, and their descendants became the bhangis. This argument fits neatly into the hindutva theory that all social evils emanate from Muslim rule, and reconstructs a glorious rajput heritage for communities like the bhangis. Such a narrative consequently downplays the role that caste has played in India.

When urbanisation set in—which should have rationally led to scientific sewage practices—Hindu society found it convenient to force madigas and bhangis into manual scavenging. When madigas from Nellore and surrounding areas were brought to other areas like Rayalaseema by the supervisors in the railways and the Public Works Department, they were not then employed for manual scavenging. They were brought along to lay the roads and the railway tracks, and later used for menial jobs. Over the last 200 years, with urbanisation, manual scavenging has entrenched itself.

The practice of manual scavenging expanded phenomenally under British rule. The British both legitimised and systematised it, while setting up army cantonments and municipalities. They created official posts of manual scavengers. All British institutions—the army, railways, courts, industries and major towns—were equipped with dry toilets instead of water-borne sewerage. The upheavals caused by commercialisation of land, destruction of artisan trades and frequent famines, pushed people out of traditional occupations and agriculture-related activities to sweeping and scavenging. This is not to say that the British invented caste or manual scavengers; rather they intervened specifically to institutionalise it. Technology is supposed to remove social prejudice; however, the technology of sanitation was structured to deepen social prejudice in India.

During and after the Partition, the Pakistani state, despite the ethnic cleansing of Hindus, refused to allow the 'untouchables' involved in safai karamchari work to emigrate to India. While the Indian government tried to secure safe passage for the Hindus of Pakistan, there was no concern about the dalit 'Hindus' left behind in Pakistan, not that a better life awaited them in India. Ambedkar raised this issue in a letter to prime minister Jawaharlal Nehru in December 1947. He expressed concern over the fact that the Pakistan government had declared sweepers as belonging to the 'Essential Services' and whom they are were not prepared to release except on one month's notice.[6]

In Andhra Pradesh, manual scavenging became a widespread practice with increasing urbanisation in the late nineteenth century. The destruction of artisan trade and imposition of property relations and commercialisation of land by the British caused social upheavals. Urbanised groups, led by the privileged castes, did not think of setting up a proper underground drainage system like the Nizam of Hyderabad did back in the 1930s. This period witnessed the importation of people to do a job that even local dalits refused to do.

Some of the dalit communities engaged in agricultural labour were gradually brought into the ambit of scavenging. In a context where the dalits were largely not allowed to own land, and where they were pushed by worsening circumstances in villages, urbanisation and the need for sweepers and scavengers was a 'pull' factor. As a result, we notice the movement of dalit communities over vast geographical distances. The methars from Haryana were brought to Telangana by the Nizam for manual scavenging. There was also substantial emigration from the Andhra region, as also within the Madras Presidency, for similar work. Madigas from Nellore went to the Tamil-speaking parts of the Presidency, and yanadis of Prakasam district came to Guntur district.[7]

Since the Nizam, Asaf Jah, maintained good relations with the British, he sent one of his officials, Mohabbat Hyder Ali, to Delhi between 1855–60 to arrange for the importation of scavenging labourers from the North.[8] The first methars came at the bidding of the Nizam and settled in Hyderabad. Soon, the methars brought over their extended families and kin to Hyderabad, and their presence gradually spread across the Telangana region with the growth of towns. The forced migration of methars from Delhi and Haryana has to be viewed in the context of similar immigration of other communities under the Nizam—a ruler who came from outside and conquered territories, and hence preferred to entrust his administration with outsiders rather than the local population. The Nizam brought in Arabs, kayasths from Uttar Pradesh, Shia Muslims from Lucknow, and Maharashtrians, Kannadigas and Tamils to run the administration. The methars thus brought in, in fact, displaced the mosalli methars—dalit converts to Islam who were scavengers in Hyderabad before the Delhi and Haryana methars came in. The madiga families of Telangana were at that time working as bonded serfs with the landlords. Whether or not scavenging was even an option for them is difficult to say given the nature of their bondage. Why did the Nizam not send for the madigas of Nellore, as did the British in Madras and Rayalaseema? Again, the complex web of relations between the ruling elite, the landed gentry and people may have dictated this, as also the natural reluctance of local, settled dalit communities (again by force, since dalit labourers were both bonded and largely unable to own land) to take up the work.

It is not as if all dalit migrants were brought in only for scavenging. When the madigas (now arundhatiyars) were brought to Tamil areas by Telugu-speaking Nayaka kings in the sixteenth and seventeenth centuries, they were not then employed for manual scavenging.[9] There was no need either, because of the absence of towns and the absence of closed dwellings without open spaces. The arundhatiyars were actually brought along to fight wars and later used for menial jobs. The yanadis of Chirala also recall that they were brought from Prakasam to lay roads and rail networks by the British, and later pushed into manual scavenging.[10] The enrolment of four people from non-scavenging dalit communities into scavenging by the Nandikotkur gram panchayat, as we shall see later in this book, also shows that poverty coupled with untouchability-by-birth can push people and communities into scavenging.

Another aspect was the natural reluctance of the untouchable castes to take up scavenging work in areas to which they belonged. The same work in a distant town would not carry the opprobrium it would locally. Hence we had rellis coming in from Orissa to the north Andhra coastal districts, East Godavari and West Godavari districts, whereas in Orissa itself, it is the ghasis and the hadis who are involved in manual scavenging.

Sewerage: A saga of neglect

Indian cities have grown in a rapid and lopsided manner. "While water supply gets votes, sewerage doesn't," says Naram Krishna Rao, retired chief engineer (public health), Government of Andhra Pradesh, who has continued to be involved in public health activities after retirement.[11] Municipalities can, for example, raise 90 percent loans from the Hyderabad Urban Development Corporation, but do not do so because councillors do not vote for sewage, they vote for water supply. Besides, the maintenance costs of the programme are high, and its benefits are not as immediately visible as they are in water supply.

This is, of course, when local bodies function at all. For the most part, however, the local government is politically and administratively unable to deal with the problems associated with unplanned and haphazard urban growth. Such inability has been fostered by various state governments all along, both by preventing local body elections for decades together, and by denying resources. Combined with corruption and inefficiency, this has in some cases reduced urban local governments almost to irrelevance.

Deteriorating urban conditions have led the growing middle class to move to new suburbs, which often have self-contained apartments and segregated living. The result is that the middle class has yet to show any real interest in, or responsibility for, pressuring governments to improve environmental conditions. While the lower classes and the urban poor politically participate in democracy, local administration is entirely subservient to state governments, which represent the interests of the middle and upper middle classes and the rich. The interests of the urban poor have really neither coalesced nor been represented by any political grouping. Various externally-funded programmes like the United Kingdom's Department for International Development slum improvement programme in Indore, which could have improved the quality of life through engineering innovations, and cleaning up the flow of untreated sewage into rivers, have foundered on the inefficiency and lack of vision of local bodies.[12]

In the absence of administrative intervention, the sewage systems themselves have grown haphazardly. In Andhra Pradesh, the seven corporations of Vijayawada, Guntur, Rajahmundry, Kurnool, Warangal, Visakhapatnam and Hyderabad, and the four municipalities of Eluru, Tenali, Nellore and Tirupati (of the 111 in the state) have only partial coverage of sewerage. Except for Tirupati which executed its sewerage programme in 1999, all the others were executed prior to 1975.[13] Public health officials therefore estimate current coverage at less than 30 percent, with the cities and towns having grown vastly during the intervening period. Hyderabad's sewerage, for example, has not seen much improvement after 1935, which explains the frequent backflow of sewage in many of the older areas of the city.

Experts like Krishna Rao say it is not advisable to have pit latrines "in rural areas where the water table is low, and within thirty feet of a water source." Similarly, he says, "septic latrines, except in isolated areas, are a public health menace, as the effluent is worse than what goes in. Sewerage and stormwater drains should never mix." Yet, all other municipalities let their sewage untreated into rivers close by. The seven municipalities around Hyderabad, for instance, including L.B. Nagar and Qutbullapur, let their sewage into the Musi river and other *nalas*[14] draining into the Musi. The individual sanitary latrines (ISLS) are thus only pretty appurtenances resting on the most terrible of sewage treatment—letting in untreated sewage in vast quantities into the local river. In many other towns and corporations, individual users connect their toilets to stormwater drains which in turn drain into the river. In Hyderabad, the entire Old City, L.B. Nagar, Kukkatpalli, Rajendranagar, Alwal and the other municipalities that surround the inner city of Hyderabad and comprise Greater Hyderabad, have such toilet outlets that drain into the Musi. Other users have septic latrines (pit latrines are not easy to maintain where the population density is high), whose repulsive outflows again enter stormwater drains causing the nasty smell found in most of these towns.

These rivers, actually drains, always pass by the poorer parts of the town. Land value is considerably less near rivers, as real estate dealers and buyers know that these rivers eventually become drains. Apart from malaria and dengue-breeding vectors, the groundwater is polluted by the river close by, from where diseases like hepatitis and gastroenteritis spread fast.

Richer neighbourhoods are relatively insulated from these dangers by expensive modern medicine, clean water (through filtering and boiling), mosquito screens and other protective mechanisms. Public health services too move relatively fast only when epidemics ravage cities. It required a plague in 1994 for sense to dawn on both the administration and people of Surat. The subsequent sanitary reform has rendered Surat the second cleanest city in India after Chandigarh.[15]

The very developments in modern medicine and civil engineering that contributed to the success of the sanitation/public health movement in nineteenth-century Britain enabled the middle class in India to largely ignore environmental problems and the resulting diseases. The use of antibiotics and insecticides have generally contained potential epidemics in slum areas, and hence not generated a general awareness among the middle class that it would be in the interest of the entire society if the poor were provided with decent living conditions.[16]

The mutual dependence between the middle class and the state has brought "a significantly higher investment in per capita terms and better maintenance of the facilities in relatively well-off areas."[17] In 1983, the national sample survey showed that around 50 percent of people in the higher income brackets had access to flush latrines that are usually connected to sewerage systems. Such systems are maintained by the local authorities. As users are only levied a nominal charge, it is easy to argue that the provision of sanitation facilities for the middle and upper classes is heavily subsidised. By contrast, fewer than 40 percent of the poor were found to have access to a latrine and about 70 percent of those with latrine facilities shared them with others.[18]

---

1   Bezwada Wilson recalls meeting a Bangladeshi from this community at the World Social Forum in Mumbai in 2004. The man's grandfather had migrated from Visakhapatnam to pre-partition Bengal.
2   R.G. Feachem, D.J. Bradley, H. Garelick and D.D.Mara, *Sanitation and Disease: Health Aspects of Excreta and Wastewater Management* (Chicester: John Wiley, 1983).
3   B.N. Srivastava, *Manual Scavenging in India: A Disgrace to the Country* (New Delhi: Concept Publishing, 1977) 16.
4   Mari Marcel Thekaekara, *Endless Filth: The Saga of the Bhangis* (Bangalore: Books for Change, 2003) 81–86.
5   N.R. Malkani, *Report of the Committee on Customary Rights to Scavenging* (New Delhi: Ministry of Home Affairs, 1965), quoted in Shyamlal, *The Bhangi: A Sweeper Caste* (Bombay: Popular Prakashan, 1992) 19.
6   See B.R. Ambedkar, *Dr. Babasaheb Ambedkar: Writings and Speeches*, vol. 17, part 1 (Mumbai: Government of Maharashtra, 2003) 369–75.
7   Answers to how and why these migrations took place are beyond the scope of this book; these questions need to be examined thoroughly by historians and activists alike.
8   Suvvada Srinivas, "Coping with Degrading Work: A study of Methars in Hyderabad City," unpublished Ph.D. thesis, (Hyderabad: Department of Anthropology, University of Hyderabad, 2003).
9   See Ravikumar, "Waiting to Lose their Patience", Introduction to *Dalits in Dravidian Land: Frontline Reports on Anti-Dalit Violence in Tamil Nadu*, (Pondicherry: Navayana Publishing, 2005) xiv.

10 Personal communication from Bezwada Wilson as also discussions with the yanadis.
11 Interview with the author, 20 September 2004.
12 Gita Dewan Verma, *Slumming India: A Chronicle of Slums and their Saviours* (New Delhi: Penguin, 2002).
13 Tirupati's sewerage programme cost Rs 35 crores. Its water supply programme cost Rs 74 crores. Information provided by the Department of Public Health, Government of Andhra Pradesh.
14 Gutters/stormwater drains are locally referred to as nalas.
15 Darshan Desai, "Khoobsurat Surat," *Outlook*, 11 October 2004.
16 Susan E. Chaplin, "Cities, sewers and poverty: India's politics of sanitation," *Environment and Urbanization*, Vol. 11, No. 1 (April 1999), 151.
17 A. Kundu, *In The Name of the Urban Poor: Access to Basic Amenities* (New Delhi: Sage, 1993).
18 Kundu, ibid.

4
Scavenging and Caste

The scandalous neglect of sewage in cities has intimate roots in the equation between excreta and 'pollution' in Hindu society. This in turn is linked, as we shall see, to caste discrimination.

In large parts of the western world, the connection between human excreta and disease is well established and accepted since at least the last two centuries. Human excreta is the principal vehicle for the transmission and spread of a wide range of communicable diseases—diarrhoea, together with malnutrition, respiratory diseases and endemic malaria are the main causes of death among children and infants in developing countries. Other infections, such as hookworm and amoebiasis cause chronic debilitating conditions that impair the quality of life and make individuals more liable to die from superimposed acute infections. In India, excreta is seen as impure. There may have been a large element of common ground between science and traditional practice. The idea may have been to help prevent the spread of fatally infectious diseases, but the notion has now calcified. Traditional practice has failed to keep up with scientific disposal of excreta, leading to skewed practices, particularly in the matter of having someone else to clean up behind us.

Excreta avoidance is ritualised: the bath is taken after defecation, and caste-Hindu parents will insist when their children are very young that children sit for defecation before the bath. The left hand is used for washing the anus, while the right hand is used for eating and other 'clean' activities. The order can never be reversed (in south

India at least). Defecation is done at a distance from the house, never inside the house, this being true until the massive urbanisation of the last five decades. Caste-Hindu society did not ever mind that public places (roads, railway tracks or wasteland) were soiled by excreta, but insisted that the inside of the house should be free of excretions. People in rural India generally avoid having toilets inside their houses, though richer sections in towns have overcome this mindset. Hence we find that wherever governments have embarked on individual toilet construction without suitable public health awareness exercises, these toilets remain unused, or are used as kitchens, storerooms or bathrooms.

Given such ritual avoidance of excreta, and the reality that excreta cannot be avoided after all, caste-Hindu society, not surprisingly, found the solution in the 'polluted' castes who would manually handle excreta. Scavenging and caste are thus intimately linked.

All South Asian countries have better sanitation access than India. The population with sustained access to improved sanitation is far less in India. Improved sanitation is defined as access to adequate excreta-disposal facilities, such as a connection to a sewer or septic tank system, a pour-flush latrine, a simple pit latrine or a ventilated improved pit latrine. An excreta-disposal system is considered adequate if it is private or shared (but not public) and if it can effectively prevent human, animal and insect contact with excreta. The figures in Table 4.1 from the United Nations Human Development Report, 2001,[1] are instructive.

For many middle-class people, the institution of manual scavenging conjures images of horror. 'A blot on humanity', 'excrescence'—are some of the terms the (English-language) media uses to describe it. While the urban elite do not directly criticise the users of the manual scavenging systems—that criticism fortunately being politically incorrect today—they resent that 'out there' there are others who get 'poor untouchables' to pick up their shit. It reaffirms the stubborn conviction that the middle class is different,

Table 4.1

HDI rank	Country	Population with sustainable access to improved sanitation (in %)	
		1990	2000
142	Pakistan	36	62
127	India	16	28
138	Bangladesh	41	48
96	Sri Lanka	85	94

and after expressing criticism and condemnation, they may sit back satisfied. Such prejudicial thinking erases our common crime—the complicity of the bulk of the middle class and a political system run by authoritarian parties to maintain economic, social and political inequality.

B.R. Ambedkar, the architect of India's Constitution, himself a dalit, dates the origin of untouchability to 400 CE.[2] The untouchable castes were not allowed to live inside towns or villages, they had to live in *kaccha* huts outside the main dwellings; they were not allowed to walk on the streets without an identifying mark: in Kerala, they had to tie a broom behind them, and a mud pot under their chin so that their polluting spit would not touch the ground;[3] in Marwar (present-day Rajasthan), the untouchables had to call out 'Payse!' ('Keep a distance!') and had to wear a crow's feather on their turban.[4] No other caste would take water or food from them. They could not intermarry. But if a man from another caste were to have an affair with one of the untouchable women, he could be forced to become a bhangi, taking on a gotra.[5]

Their humiliation in numerous ways has persisted. In Metharwadi in the Sultan Shahi area of the Old City of Hyderabad, the elderly hesitate to mention their names. On insistence, they retort:

> What do you want to know? We were told very categorically by the upper castes that our names were to be self-ridiculing.

If any parent or grandparent chose a fair name for the child, we were instantly abused for having lost sight of our *aukath* (social and moral position). Yes, write down the names, they are—Jhamta (spade), Kaloo (black), Gobar (dung), Tawa (black griddle), Bhiku Ram (beggar), Ghoodo (horse), Phullo, Matutva and Tatutva, Dhappo, Bhetari, Anguri (grapes) etc. Our names were the first insight into our identity.[6]

The men's names segregate them as lesser humans and the women's suggest sexual ridicule.

The turn of the twentieth century brought unexpected changes. While British rule helped institutionalise manual scavenging in towns instead of bringing in modern sanitation, it also freed dalits from "a destiny preordained by the Hindu God and enforced by the Hindu State".[7] The East India Company needed soldiers, employed untouchables and enforced compulsory education for all Indian soldiers and their children. With education and nontraditional employment, dalits began to stir. By the 1930s, it had become clear that the dalits were beginning to assert their rights under the leadership of Dr B.R. Ambedkar. Hinduism reacted to the new dalit threat in two important ways. Militant Hinduism began to incorporate the dalits into a *shuddhi* (purification–conversion) and *sangathan* (consolidation) movement to denude the notion of dalit independence. Mohandas Gandhi, on the other hand, held out the hand of charity to the dalits and attempted to help individuals among them, setting up the Harijan Sevak Sangh in 1932 (which incidentally excluded untouchables), and beginning the publication of *Harijan*. Ambedkar viewed Gandhi's moves as 'killing untouchables with kindness'. Gandhi's 'Harijan tour' of 1933–34 brought the issue of untouchability into the nationalist mainstream. Gandhi insisted that dalits should not secure their rights by satyagraha. Both at the Round Table Conference in London in 1931, and during the Poona Pact discussions in 1932, Gandhi claimed that he was the rightful leader of the untouchables.

At the heart of the gandhian discourse on caste was the romanticisation of the bhangi and her work.[8] "The bhangi," Gandhi wrote in 1936, "constitutes the foundation of all services. A bhangi does for society what a mother does for her baby. A mother washes her baby of the dirt and insures his health. Even so the bhangi protects and safeguards the health of the entire community by maintaining sanitation for it."[9]

Further: "I love scavenging ... I do not want to be reborn. But if I have to be reborn, I should be born an untouchable, so that I may share their sorrows, sufferings and the affronts levelled at them, in order that I may endeavour to free myself and them from that miserable condition."[10] Gandhi chastises the unwilling sweeper: "You should realise that you are cleaning Hindu Society." Ambedkar's call to the dalits to give up traditional, polluting practices was countered by Gandhi who argued that scavenging work was 'protective' of the sanitation of the entire society. No doubt, Gandhi had in mind the disturbing trend of sweepers' strikes all over the country—in Batala (Punjab, 1926), in Calcutta (1928), in Kabul and Jalandhar (1937), and a nationwide strike of sweepers led by the communists in the 1940s.[11] "The Bhangis may not go on strike for lack of amenities," urged Gandhi.[12]

Even while encouraging nondalits to take up scavenging, Gandhi was averse to those born as scavengers giving up the profession or expressing protest against the indignities they were made to suffer. Ambedkar's understanding struck at the root of the gandhian premise.[13]

> Under Hinduism scavenging was not a matter of choice, it was a matter of force. What does Gandhism do? It seeks to perpetuate this system by praising scavenging as the noblest service to society! ... What is the use of telling the scavenger that even a Brahmin is prepared to do scavenging when it is clear that according to Hindu Shastras and Hindu notions even if a Brahmin did scavenging he would never be subject to the disabilities of one who is a born scavenger? For in India a man is not a scavenger because of his work. He is a scavenger because of his birth irrespective of the question whether he does scavenging or not.[14]

If the views of Ambedkar had prevailed on the scavenging castes, as they did on a large section of other dalits, it is likely that manual scavenging may have had an early demise in India.[15] Ambedkar was categorical that dalits must shun unclean occupations such as scavenging and turn to education, organisation and agitation. Gandhi's views on scavenging, on the other hand, fit into his base among the caste Hindus, and his natural impulse to carry them along with him. However, little genuine change has taken place, unless those suffering from its lack impel it.

---

1   Source: http://hdr.undp.org/statistics/data/indic/indic_60_1_1.html, accessed on 6 June 2005.
2   B.R. Ambedkar, *The Untouchables: Who were they and why they became Untouchables?* in *Dr. Babasaheb Ambedkar: Writings and Speeches*, Vol. 7 (Mumbai: Government of Maharashtra, 1990) 379.
3   Chentanassery, *Ayyankali*, accessed at www.ambedkar.org on 12 April 2005.
4   L.S.S.O. Molley, *Indian Caste Customs* (Delhi: Vikas, 1974) 150, quoted in Shyamlal, ibid., 25.
5   Shyamlal, ibid., 66–67.
6   Jatiram, Baneer Singh and Phulan when interviewed by Vimala in Metharwadi on 12 and 20 September 2004.
7   B.R. Ambedkar, *What Congress and Gandhi have done to the Untouchables*, in *Dr. Babasaheb Ambedkar: Writings and Speeches*, Vol. 9 (Mumbai: Government of Maharashtra, 1990) 189.
8   For an overview of Gandhi's approach to the issue of scavengers and scavenging, see Appendix 4, 'Mohandas Gandhi on Scavenging' of this book, 86–95.
9   M.K. Gandhi, "The Ideal Bhangi," *Harijan*, 28 November 1936, in *Collected Works of Mahatma Gandhi*, vol. LXIV, 86–88.
10 *Young India*, 27 April 1921.
11 For an account, see Prashad, *Untouchable Freedom*, 132. Between 1936–40, municipal workers were organised by the Communist Party in Kakinada, Gudivada, Guntur, Eluru, Tenali, Vijayawada, Machilipatnam and Nellore. A conference of municipal workers was held in Nellore in August 1939, where three broad demands were framed

for the movement. These were: i) carts should be drawn by oxen, not by scavengers; ii) scavengers should have to clean individual dry toilets in only forty houses, not hundred, as was the rule then; iii) women should be paid equal wages as men, employment should be made permanent, there should be holidays, provision of provident fund, and the then GO saying that more than Rs 12 per month could not be paid to municipal workers should be abolished. See Y.V.Krishna Rao, Tummala Venkatramaiah, Etukuri Balaramamurthy, Parakala Pattabhirama Rao, *Andhra Pradesh Communist Party Udhyamacharitra, 1936–42*, Vol. II (Vijayawada: Visalandhra Publishing House, 1988). The Andhra Pradesh Municipal Workers' Union was formed in 1941.

12 *Harijan*, 12 May 1946.
13 For an overview of Ambedkar's approach to the issue of scavengers and scavenging, see Appendix 5, 'Ambedkar on Scavenging' of this book, 96–106.
14 *Congress and Gandhi*, 292.
15 The reason why Ambedkar made a relatively weak impression is that the bhangis were closely associated with the Congress. The fissures between the chamars led by Mangu Ram and the balmikis led by Chunni Lal contributed to this. Since mid-1920s various organisations of dalits came up in India. The All India Jati Sudhar Mahasabha was formed in 1922, and the Adi-Dharm Mandal a little later. There was a clash of respective caste heritages, as the chamars revered Ravidas and the chuhras (balmikis) revered Valmiki. In 1927, the balmikis formed their own Balmiki Ad Dharm Mandal. There was a concerted effort by caste-Hindu reformers like Gauri Shankar Acharya, Ami Chand and Sadhu Yodhnath to link the balmikis with militant Hinduism. Ami Chand, in fact, composed *Valmiki Prakash* in 1936, which is even today the staple tract of the balmikis all over India. The efforts of Hindu militants and gandhians paid dividends and the bhangis of north India remained largely alienated from Ambedkar's movement.

5
What Has Been Done to Stop Scavenging?

The manual scavengers, particularly bhangis, did not identify with the dalit movement initiated and inspired by Ambedkar. In north India, the chamars have been the mainstay of the dalit movement, with the bhangis preferring to remain with the Congress. In south India, the scavengers belong to various communities—the madigas, rellis and yanadis.

Briefly during the 1940s, the sanitation workers in coastal Andhra were organised into a Municipal Workers' Union, with the support of the Communist Party and led by L.V. Ratnam (a nondalit). In 1945–46, this union organised a strike by manual scavengers for higher wages.[1] While the strike could not be sustained for more than two to three days in the rest of coastal Andhra, it lasted about thirty days in Nellore till the municipality agreed to the demands.[2] After this brief period, the madigas largely remained with the Congress as also the rellis and the yanadis.[3] Since the late 1980s, the dalit movement began making inroads into the scavenger community too. After the 1984 Karamchedu massacre,[4] a coherent and strong dalit movement emerged in Andhra Pradesh. Earlier, there had been active organisations such as the SC Employees' Welfare Association and Ambedkar Yuvajana Sangham, but after the Karamchedu massacre many activists of these organisations and others came forward to form and support the Dalit Mahasabha. The Dalit Mahasabha worked on the Karamchedu and Chunduru[5] massacres and various other issues. In the early 1990s, there was a downswing in the activities of the Mahasabha and it suffered a major split. This was almost immediately followed by a political division between the malas and madigas, resulting from the failure of the dalit movement to critically address the question of inequalities and hierarchies within dalit communities. Recent developments in the dalit movement indicate a rapid NGO-isation. It was in this period of a 'low' that the Safai Karamchari Andolan (SKA) was formed, and it organised the scavenging community with the broad support of all dalits. The SKA, of course, has taken Ambedkar's vision directly to the scavengers.

After independence, various state governments and the union government established commissions and committees to look into the issue. The then Government of Bombay appointed the Scavengers' Living Conditions Enquiry Committee headed by V.N. Barve in 1949, which submitted its report in 1952.[6] The Barve Committee did not ask for abolition of dry toilets, but instead for the amelioration of the working conditions of scavengers. The N.R. Malkani Committee was appointed in 1957 by the Central Advisory Board of Harijan Welfare, which itself was constituted in 1956 under the Ministry of Home Affairs. The Committee, known as the Scavenging Conditions Inquiry Committee, submitted its report in 1960, largely recommending ameliorative measures again. The Central Department of Social Welfare appointed a second committee in 1965, again under the chairmanship of N.R. Malkani, to examine the abolition of the 'customary rights' of the scavengers. The I.P.D. Salappa Committee in Karnataka released its report, *Improvement of Living and Working Conditions of Sweepers and Scavengers*, in 1976. All these committees, while highlighting the pitiable conditions of the scavengers, recommended ameliorative measures, not abolition.

In 1969, the union government took up a special programme for converting dry toilets into water-pour flush latrines. Under this programme, a 25 percent subsidy and a 75 percent loan was offered.[7] The Union Ministry of Works and Housing gave loans to convert dry latrines to pour-flush ones under its Integrated Development of

Small and Medium Towns scheme. The Housing and Urban Development Corporation (HUDCO) also financed loans to local bodies. It was Bindeshwar Pathak's Sulabh Shouchalaya scheme, which means a 'simple latrine', initiated in 1974, that heralded a slow change in the system. The twin-pit pour-flush toilet was cost effective, consumed less water and had indigenous material and know-how. With the twin pits working alternately and continuously, composting on-site was possible, and complete desludging was pathogen-free, unlike in a single-pit toilet. Pathak was given several awards, generously feted by international agencies, and his toilet was taken up by several state governments.[8] In an internationally funded endeavour, Pathak set up Sulabh Shouchalayas all over India in major towns. These are now common enough sights at metropolitan bus stands, railway stations and public places. They are, however, almost completely staffed by members of the scavenging community. Pathak envisions the 'liberation' of scavengers from manual scavenging but not from the caste and the profession in a new form. The Sulabh toilet mirrors the caste system. The caretaker (who does not soil his hands) is usually a caste Hindu and a Bihari; he is paid a salary between Rs 1,500 to Rs 2,000 per month. The caretaker also collects money from users and supervises the actual cleaners, either bhangis or madigas who work in a shift system and are paid Rs 600 to Rs 900 per month.[9] The Sulabh endeavour has not been able to break the stranglehold of the caste system on occupations.

While Pathak's Sulabh Shouchalaya was a viable alternative to the dry toilet, the stage was set for the criminalisation of the dry toilet itself in the Employment of Manual Scavengers and Construction of Dry Latrines (Prohibition) Act, 1993, whch defines a scavenger as "a person engaged in or employed for manually carrying human excreta."[10] This Act bans scavenging. Section 3 says "no person shall a) engage in or employ or permit to be engaged in or employed for any other person for manually carrying human excreta; or b) construct or maintain a dry latrine."

Section 14 prescribes the punishment for doing so: "Whoever fails to comply with or contravenes any of the provisions of this Act... shall in respect of each failure or contravention be punishable with imprisonment for a term which may extend to one year or with fine, which may extend to two thousand rupees or with both, and in case the failure or contravention continues, with additional fine which may extend to one hundred rupees every day."

While the Act was given assent to by the president in 1993, it did not come into force till 24 January 1997 in Andhra Pradesh when the Department of Urban Development, Ministry of Urban Affairs and Employment, which spearheaded the Act in parliament, actually notified it in the Gazette of India. The same was the case in Maharashtra, Karnataka, Goa, Tripura and West Bengal and the union territories. While most states in India have adopted the Act,[11] some like Rajasthan and Uttar Pradesh have not yet adopted it; others like Kerala, Nagaland and Pondicherry assert that there is not need to adopt the Act despite statistics showing the existence of dry toilets in these states. According to official records, Kerala has 1,339 dry toilets; Nagaland 1,800; and Pondicherry 476.[12] Andhra Pradesh formally adopted the Act only in 2001.[13]

The National Commission for Safai Karamcharis was constituted in 1994 to monitor the situation and recommend specific programmes. The National Safai Karamchari Finance and Development Corporation (NSKFDC) was formed in 1997, as an apex institution for the all-round socioeconomic uplift of safai karamcharis and to extend financial assistance to them for income generation and viable projects. The National Human Rights Commission (NHRC) has also taken cognisance of the issue.[14] In one of NHRC's meetings with the union government, it was agreed that manual scavenging should be eradicated by 2 October 2002.[15]

In Andhra Pradesh, no department in the government deals directly with the issue of manual scavenging. The Commissioner of Panchayat Raj oversees the gram panchayats that are the major offenders in carrying out manual scavenging. The director, Municipal

Administration, oversees the municipalities that also employ manual scavengers. Sewerage in an item of least concern to these public bodies; water supply is considered far more important. The Department of Social Welfare supervises the welfare of scavengers who are Scheduled Castes. The Andhra Pradesh Scheduled Castes Cooperative Finance Corporation (APSCCFC), also known as the SC Corporation, is the apex body which is in charge of the AP Government's Mission to Eradicate Manual Scavenging; its managing director is the member-convener of the Mission.

Officials have mixed views—alternatives should be presented to users before demolition. Where will users go, especially women? To worsen the dilemma, the actual demolition of the dry toilets cannot be done by the Mission or the APSCCFC; municipalities and gram panchayats have to do it in their respective areas. There is also much opposition from local users to demolition in the absence of alternative sanitary initiatives. The SKA records that the executive officer of the gram panchayat of Kallur, a small town in Kurnool district, was beaten up by users for attempting to demolish the community dry latrine (CDL). No mechanism of the government protects these minor officials from public anger. In 2003, J.C. Sharma, managing director of APSCCFC, had participated in a demolition of a CDL in Hyderabad. He recalls that of the roughly twenty-five families using the toilet, twenty had already constructed individual sanitary latrines (ISLs); the remaining five came and lay down outside the toilet in protest against the demolition.[16] Similarly, he recalls that a demolition was stopped after an MLA protested in West Godavari district.

Rehabilitation

The Andhra Pradesh government set up the Mission to Eradicate Manual Scavenging in 2001 to rehabilitate scavengers. The rehabilitation schemes covered theoretically all scavengers belonging to the Scheduled Caste community in urban areas, semi-urban areas and rural areas. There was no age limit for the beneficiaries of rehabilitation. However, for the purpose of training in various trades, the age limit was set as 15–50 years by the government. The duration of the training of identified scavengers and their dependents ranged from one month to six months. The training institutes set up by the union government, state governments and union territory administrations implemented training programmes and the entire cost was borne by the union government. The state government used the training centres, infrastructure and facilities created for training in various trades by different departments of the state governments, while the union government used the ones set up by non-governmental organisations. For other self-employment schemes meant for rehabilitation of scavengers, the executive directors of APSCCFC could identify schemes of (approximately) Rs 1 lakh and communicate to the head office immediately to finalise an action plan for implementation of a comprehensive programme. The funding pattern of such schemes is 50 percent subsidy (that is, an outright grant to a maximum of Rs 10,000), 20 percent margin money (this is an outright subsidy to the beneficiary) and the balance as a loan from NSKFDC. The scheme was implemented strictly for those scavengers who were already identified by the district societies of the APSCCFC during the August 2000 Janmabhoomi programme.[17] While no reservation target was set for women, the corporation estimates that about 45 percent of the beneficiaries have been women.[18]

In practice, however, rehabilitation went along entirely different lines.[19] Several schemes such as buffalo-rearing, garments stores, petty shop business, vegetable vending and auto-driving were conceived as rehabilitation schemes at outlays of Rs 50,000 and above. The bank loan was Rs 32,000, Rs 10,000 was the loan component from the SC Corporation, and Rs 8,000 was the grant component from the same Corporation.[20] Banks, however, refused to lend—continuing to treat the scavengers as untouchables.[21] Troubled with meeting targets, local officials of the APSCCFC devised a truly ingenious plan: each beneficiary was given Rs 8,000 (of which Rs 2,000 went to the broker/agent, and Rs 500 to Rs 600 towards paperwork), the loan component was shown as 'recovered', and everybody was happy. In other words, the asset was simply absent, except on paper. The beneficiaries were not always scavengers—the actual scavengers were, in the perception of the authorities and bankers, old, illiterate and unable to even show a change of occupation on paper. The older safai karamcharis were discriminated against as being unfit for rehabilitation. As in several government schemes, non-safai karamcharis reaped financial benefits. Younger members of the scavenging family, and other smarter non-safai karamchari members of the community were shown as beneficiaries. The scavengers continued to scavenge, the users were happy, and the dry toilets remained.

It requires more imaginative planning to rehabilitate scavengers in a local society that will consider them scavengers for years to come. To expect a largely illiterate community to take to dairying, petty business, vegetable vending and other such enterprises, and withstand competition from well-established traditional traders demonstrates the planners' insensitivity and lack of commitment to genuine reform. More sensible options would be the outright purchase or grant of two acres of cultivable land, or a government job. However, none of these schemes, either singly or jointly, has been able to completely address the problem of dry toilets, both individual and community.

---

1   Interview with Prof K. Seshadri (20 September 2004), a communist activist in Nellore, who later taught Political Science at various universities.

2   Seshadri recalls that there was intense activity during the strike. There were processions every second day, with the slogan *Paki karmikulaku nyayam jaragali!* ('Justice for the scavenger employees!'). The strike notice was given to the municipality a month in advance. He recalls that there was surprising sympathy from the users, largely the middle class. At this time, wages for the manual scavengers were being paid directly by the municipality, who in turn levied charges on the users. Nellore town began to stink and officials feared an outbreak of cholera. However, there was clandestine scavenging with users personally paying the

scavengers to work every second day. The municipality finally agreed to raise the wages for the scavengers.

3   When Seshadri was asked why the madigas shifted to the Congress, he said that this was part of the general development. The Congress had power, could promise and deliver largesse, whereas the Communists could only lead struggles, which became more and more difficult to sustain.

4   On 17 July 1985, six dalit men were murdered and three dalit women raped by the kammas in Karamchedu, Prakasam district. The Dalit Mahasabha was formed in response to this incident.

5   On 6 August 1991, eight dalits were murdered by the reddys in Chunduru, 40 km from Guntur, and their bodies were disposed in gunnysacks. After the Karamchedu massacre, Chunduru became a rallying point for the dalit movement in Andhra Pradesh.

6   Srivastava, ibid., 35.

7   Later, several other schemes came into vogue, all centrally-funded.

8   Bindeshwar Pathak became active in the field in the 1960s, following the Gandhi centenary, when the Bihar government decided to give 50 percent of the total cost of construction of pour-flush latrines as grant. In 1974, the Bihar government allowed the funds to be spent by Sulabh International which claims to have converted 1.86 lakh of the 4 lakh dry latrines into sanitary ones between 1974–88 in Bihar alone.

9   These workers are certainly not paid better than the permanently employed manual scavengers in state-run municipalities. For instance, a permanent employee in Dhone municipality in Andhra Pradesh earns Rs 4,030 a month. However, state-run municipalities have, since the past decade, stopped further employment of permanent workers, and vacancies are simply not filled. Instead, sanitation works are contracted out to private agencies who again employ either madigas or bhangis at about the same wage paid by Sulabh. Of late, in Hyderabad, other castes and communities such as the gypsy lambadas are also seeking employment in sanitation work.

10 The Act was spearheaded by the Ministry of Urban Development and passed in the interests of urban sanitation and fuelled by international concerns, and less because of concern for scavengers. For the full text of the Act, see Appendix 2 of this book, 74–83.

11 Central Acts of parliament have to be adopted by the state legislatures. Appropriate rules have to be framed for an Act. Till this is done, despite the notification of the Act, state governments do not generally implement it.

12 Chart prepared with manual scavengers in each state by the Union Ministry of Social Justice and Empowerment for 2002–03.
13 GO Ms No. 75 dated 28 August 2001.
14 NHRC Annual Report 2001–02 devotes a page to the issue.
15 It is ironic that Gandhi's birth anniversay is set as a deadline. It has become part of official common sense to associate any effort at the eradication of manual scavenging with Gandhi while he was in fact opposed to such moves. See Appendix 4 of this book for a sampling of Gandhi's views on manual scavenging.
16 Interview with the author, 15 September 2005. In 2003, Sharma supervised the demolition of a dry toilet in the Old City of Hyderabad.
17 Janmabhoomi, the pet scheme of N. Chandrababu Naidu, former Telugu Desam Party chief minister (1995–2004), was shelved by the new Congress Government in May 2004. Launched in January 1997, the Janmabhoomi scheme invited people to participate in development works. It focused on contribution of labour by citizens towards construction of schools, health centres and also focused on family welfare (read family planning), environment, conservation and responsive governance.
18 Information given by APSCCFC in a personal communication.
19 This was evident from discussions at Chirala, Nandikotkur, and with several groups of manual scavengers who attended the rally on 16 September 2004 in Hyderabad, from different parts of the state. This impression was also supported by Wilson.
20 As the NSKFDC subsidy of 50 percent was only upto a maximum limit of Rs 10,000, and since workable schemes needed more money, this was the plan worked out by the APSCCFC.
21 In each area, certain banks are designated as lead banks. These banks do the lending to tailor with government welfare programmes. It is generally reported by beneficiaries in most welfare programmes (DRDA, DWCRA, disabled welfare, farmer's loans, loans for SCS STS and OBCS) that the banks are uncooperative. There is clear tension between the banks' notion of 'bankability' which, in peripheral areas, means the capacity to pay back irrespective of the success or failure of the scheme, and the welfare notion that people need a helping hand and some capital to work.

6

How Widespread is Manual Scavenging Today?

As cited at the beginning of this book, statistics released by the Union Ministry of Social Justice and Empowerment for 2002–03, reveal that there are 6.76 lakh manual scavengers in the country, spread over twenty-one states and union territories, working at 96 lakh dry latrines. The National Commission for Safai Karamcharis, in its third report in 2000, noted that manual scavengers were employed in the military engineering services, army, public sector undertakings and the Indian Railways. Thirty dry latrines in Golconda in Hyderabad (under the army) were converted, while eighteen still await the process of conversion. Cities like Delhi (trans-Jamuna), Shimla, Mathura, Agra, Bhopal, Jaipur and Indore have a high concentration of dry toilets.

In Andhra Pradesh alone, the number of individual dry latrines (in private houses) was estimated to be between two and three lakh,[1] while CDLs maintained by municipalities and gram panchayats were estimated at 25,762.[2] Kurnool tops all the districts with 4,782 CDLs, Anantapur comes second (4,173) followed by West Godavari (3,505) and East Godavari (2,248). Visakhapatnam and Cuddapah are major offenders with 2,251 and 2,324 respectively.[3] This enumeration has been possible because of the extraordinary cooperation between the Safai Karamchari Andolan and the AP Scheduled Caste Cooperative Finance Corporation, which resulted in a unique survey of dry toilets in Andhra Pradesh. The state government wanted to declare the state the first dry-toilet-free one in December 2002. The timeframe has been extended to December 2005. The deadline is impractical given that after the initial momentum—following the survey report and the establishment of the Mission—the state and its machinery have lapsed into lethargy. The Mission is vested with the task of eradicating dry toilets, but the responsibility for the actual demolition rests with the other departments—the Department of Panchayat Raj for gram panchayats, and the Department of Municipal Administration for municipalities.

We must also remember that apart from dry latrines, the manual cleaning of pit and septic latrines constitutes an offence under the Act. This has not been enumerated. However, in all small towns and villages manual cleaning of pit and septic latrines goes on routinely. Similarly, the entire railway network is that of dry toilets, with manual cleaning at railway stations. At bus stands, since running water is not available, a similar situation prevails. Due to the haphazard growth of towns and cities, large numbers of the urban poor defecate on the main roads, which also require daily manual cleaning. Even theatres in Kurnool district have dry latrines which require cleaning.

Appendix 3 gives a detailed list of hitherto enumerated CDLs maintained by the gram panchayats and municipalities. The basic fieldwork for this was done in 2001, but it was not comprehensive, which means that it is likely that the list is longer. Moreover, some of the latrines have been demolished or converted by the authorities in the intervening period.

In the following pages, we present 'snapshots' from three locations in Andhra Pradesh where dry latrines and manual scavenging have been a part of daily life.

Chirala

Chirala, in Prakasam district, located 5 km from the coast, is a municipality with a population of about 82,000. It has been a centre for handloom weaving for centuries. In coastal Andhra manual scavengers are referred to as *paki* workers, a derogatory term that the scavenging community has internalised. The workers are largely yanadis, a Scheduled Tribe, and a sprinkling of madigas. Not surprisingly, there is a fair amount of denial here.[4] It takes time, and gaining of confidence, to get people to admit that they are engaged in the cleaning human excreta. Very few local sanitation workers participated in the procession through the town—they wouldn't have wanted to be marked by the local population. Many of the activists were from Ongole, where the SKA has successfully organised the local manual scavengers in demolishing three of the town's CDLS earlier.

With the increase in the number of pour-flush toilets, the scavengers have been guided into yet another line of this work. Rapuru Kotaiah and Chenchamma, Eluru Pedda Anjaiah and Potluri Subbamma, all in their mid-sixties now, recall the days when they manually cleaned both IDLS and CDLS. They used a piece of tin to lift the excrement into a woven basket lined with leaves to prevent leakage. They carried the basket on their shoulders to a place far away where all such refuse was dumped.

Today, their children and grandchildren are in the same profession. Kotaiah's three adult sons (and his educated grandson) work at cleaning septic latrines. They work in a team of ten, with six buckets and as many drums as rickshaws. One of them, always a man, consumes a good amount of alcohol before commencing work. Kerosene is poured on the surface of the sludge when the lid of the septic tank is opened—to enable the absorption of poisonous gases—and then the man enters with the bucket into the solid mass of excreta. Another lifts the bucket up, and this is passed by the human chain to the drum waiting in the rickshaw.

Kotamma says that the work is done only in the dark. "Everybody shits, but who wants to see it? So we work in the night." What do they think of a system that forces one group of human beings to clean other humans' excreta? They are bitter, "We soil ourselves, so that others can look clean," says she. They don't take their daughters to work, only their daughters-in-law. "Our daughters will anyway go to households where they will have to do this work. God permit, they may go into households with other occupations. Let them be free of this at least now," they say. They experience a very physical form of untouchability in everyday life: shopkeepers will not take money from their hands; the money is put on a counter, water is sprinkled on it, and only then taken.

The community may be in the business of cleaning, but they are not allowed to take up domestic work such as cleaning houses and washing vessels. They are only expected to clean human waste. Some work as contract labourers to clean latrines in public places such as the bus stand and the railways station. Here too, manual lifting of excreta is unavoidable. The lack of running water, or sometimes the total non-availability of water, leaves users to shit all over the place. Many, like Potluri Narayanamma, work in hospitals and nursing homes, again as people who clean latrines and mop the excreta, urine, blood and the waste after a delivery.

After a lifetime of carrying the waste of 'decent folk', these people still remain desperately poor. They live in tiny thatched-leaf huts with minimal belongings. They have no electricity. In Ujilipet, for instance, there is a single tap for about twenty-three households, and only three toilets, recently built; the rest squat by the railway track a kilometre away. Most of them cannot afford to pay Rs 250, the necessary beneficiary contribution to be paid at the outset for getting the government to construct a toilet; nor do they have the time and energy required for running behind municipal officials.[5]

Nandikotkur

Till 2003, Nandikotkur, in Kurnool district, had nearly a thousand dry toilets, all serviced by the permanent employees of the gram panchayat.[6] The latter collected service charges of Rs 15 once in three months, and the house owners paid a little extra to the manual scavengers to encourage them to come every day to clean. There are presently eighteen permanent employees (eleven women, seven men) and twenty-six temporary employees (twelve women, fourteen men). The entire class of permanent sweepers in the gram panchayats are madigas with a small sprinkling of malas from Nellore district. There were twenty-two CDLS, of which five were demolished in 2003 by the executive officer of the gram panchayat, following the first drive of the APSCCFC and the SKA. The demolition of the other dry latrines was stopped in 2003 when the users made a representation to the then MLA[7] and the collector, who stopped further demolition. Given the conflict between various arms of the government, the APSCCFC simply sidestepped the issue and avoided precipitation of further conflict. There were still seventeen CDLS cleaned by the permanent employees until 8 August 2004 when the SKA entered the picture.

On 8 August 2004, the SKA partially demolished the CDL at Patabandlarasta near Shikarpet. The permanent employees refused to continue manual scavenging now that they knew the law and had the support of the SKA. They were invited for negotiations by the executive officer and the sarpanch even as the gram panchayat informally engaged four workers (three madigas and one halalkhor), supposed to be paid by the people themselves for one month until alternative arrangements were made. Local reporters, however, told us that the proposal by the gram panchayat for the conversion of three CDLS at an estimated Rs 15 lakh had been turned down by the collector because of paucity of funds. None of the newly recruited manual scavengers had been engaged in such work; they were agricultural labourers. They had joined in the hope that once they took up this work and got a foothold in the gram panchayat, they could eventually gain regular employment in the cleaning of drains, sweeping, and such tasks. Hazrath, a madiga sanitation worker and an enthusiastic convert to the SKA's drive, asked Ma Basha, one of the halalkhor workers: "The other three are madigas; why do you want to get into this work?" The worker showed him his hovel, pointed to his four little daughters, and Hazrath kept quiet.

Immediately after the partial demolition of one of the seventeen CDLS, all permanent employees ceased manual scavenging. For eight days the remaining four undemolished toilets lay uncleaned, and the town began stinking. There was much resentment among the users. All political groups, including the Communist Party of India, the Communist Party of India (Marxist) and New Democracy (a Marxist–Leninist faction), demanded that the gram panchayat either continue the old practice of manual scavenging or create new facilities. It took the demolition of the dry latrines for them to make this demand. Prior to the SKA agitation, no group or party, irrespective of its ideological affiliation, considered the issue of manual scavenging from the point of the view of the scavengers.

Hazrath is 33 years, and his body language and direct gaze proclaim him a natural leader. He is a madiga from Duttaluru village near Udayagiri town, Nellore district. Hazrath's ancestors had migrated as scavengers and sweepers to other parts of the country; he has relatives in places as distant as Shimoga (Karnataka) and Goa. From what he recalls, it was the British who arranged this migration of sweepers. When he was young, he was hesitant to join this work. He dropped out of school to join the CPI(M) and recalls roaming all of Andhra Pradesh on party work. When he married in 1985, he took up masonry, but his father-in-law's death in 1993 pushed him into the profession of sweeping. His father-in-law dying in service allowed any other family member to become eligible for the post, a permanent one. More so than in other professions, the sweeper jobs are by default hereditary; because of the distasteful work, other castes shun it. If Hazrath had not taken it, the job would have passed out of the family. Later, he educated his only sister-in-law to M.A., LLB.

Why did he join this profession? "No one told us that it was wrong, no one told us that we did not have to do it. Do you think we wanted to do it? We were afraid we would lose our jobs. Then came Wilson to tell us that we must stop the work, it was illegal and inhuman. He was there with us, come what may. All we required was that little help."[8] (He met Wilson only on 8 August 2004.) Hazrath draws a startling comparison: "Even if god is good, if the priest is bad, it does not help people. If the priest is good, the cries of people will reach god. Earlier we had no network, no support. Now, after Wilson's campaign, even the authorities are frightened to ask us to clean shit. They will only request us. They dare not force us."

Except for the permanent staff, the women who constitute the NMRS (non-muster roll employees who actually are contract workers), are paid only Rs 900 per month, their payment coming once in three months. At the time of writing this in October 2004, the Government of Andhra Pradesh represented by its gram panchayat, owed them two months' wages. The executive officer of the gram panchayat said he could do little since it is the government that pays the salary bill. While employees of Classes I, II and III are paid fairly promptly, Class IV staff are paid once in three or four months. Consequently, they borrow heavily at annual interest rates that range from 36 percent to 60 percent.

Of the sweepers who functioned as manual scavengers till less than a month ago, we met Sowbhagyamma and Devdas, both permanent workers. Sowbhagyamma, 48, came to Nandikotkur thirty-five years ago owing to her marriage. Her husband also works in the gram panchayat as a sweeper. She was appointed to a *thotti* post, the south Andhra Telugu term for manual scavenger. She is taciturn, and has just one thing to say about the work she has done for 35 years: "I don't like it."

Devdas is more voluble. "We lifted thirty to forty baskets full of shit, which the women heaped and left outside the CDL, into the tractor. Four of us accompanied the tractor which stopped some distance away from the compost pit. We carried the baskets to the field and threw the shit there. Our hands, legs, clothes ... all were dirtied with the shit. I will never do this work again. Never. Even if they dismiss me from service, I will take up some other manual labour. Though I don't smoke, I have asthma, and the doctor says that this is because of my work all these years."

From the accounts of the sweepers, it seems as if most of the actual scavenging work at the dry toilets is done by women. The baskets are then picked up by the men, taken to the tractor, and in it to the compost field where it is emptied by them.

Hyderabad

Hyderabad, the capital of Andhra Pradesh, is a bustling 400-year-old city with a population of seven million. (The population of Inner Hyderabad alone is 4.2 million.) The city's history began with the establishment of the Qutb Shahi dynasty in 1591. The famous Charminar marks the centre of the Old City, from where the city grew along the river Musi.

A sewerage system was in place and in use over 150 years ago in Hyderabad under the Qutb Shahi dynasty. With urbanisation, the civic needs of the population increased, especially since the social elite among both Muslims and Hindus practised purdah or female seclusion. Purdah was practised by kayasths, khatris, rajputs and deccanis among the Hindus, and Muslims of Persian, Arab and Mughal descent among the Muslims. This led to the construction of dry latrines in the backyards of households inhabited by the ruling classes.

The migrant methar community claim that dry latrines in the Old City were initially cleaned by a section among Muslims known as mosalli methars and by local balmiki castes (scavenging castes of Telugu origin) known derogatorily as dheds/madigas. Many dalits embraced Islam in Hyderabad and were known as deccani or mosalli methars.[9] Though the Muslim community did not treat them with as much contempt as the Hindus had done, conversion to Islam did not enable them to sever the link with their previous caste-based occupation.[10]

Given the long history of social exclusion and abuse by caste Hindus, the elderly balmikis in Metharwadi point out that they were treated more humanely by their Muslim clients. "We are offered tea in the same cups, there is no restriction applied on us entering their homes, the money is paid in our hands and not placed on the ground," says Baneer Singh, one of the methar elders whose grandfather had migrated to Hyderabad. "I am lucky that I served many Muslim households." However, class-based exclusion was in practice among Muslims for the converted mosalli methars and for methars in general, and this attitude prevails.

Baneer Singh, 65, insists that his family had never been involved in human faeces disposal in their ancestral village in Haryana. However, they were aware of the nature of the work that awaited them in Hyderabad from neighbours whose family members had already migrated. Baneer Singh's grandfather decided to migrate at the turn of the twentieth century with the entire family, and all the members of the family were engaged in manual scavenging. Baneer Singh, who was born in Hyderabad, eventually secured a scavenging job with the Municipal Corporation of Hyderabad (MCH) and his wife continues to work as a scavenger with the police department. Of his thirteen children, two sons are working as private scavengers.

Both men and women were engaged in scavenging in Hyderabad. However, since it was the social seclusion of women belonging to privileged caste/class groups women that demanded the need for in-house dry latrines for these women, balmiki women formed the greater majority of individual household dry latrine cleaners. The Nizam's princely state was annexed to the Indian Union in 1949 and since then public sanitation became the responsibility of the MCH. This led to the setting up of official posts for cleaning public latrines, streets and drains. It was balmiki men, rather than their wives, who clamoured to fill these ranks. Better salaries, job security and the attendant benefits were considered the prerogative of men in a typically patriarchal manner.

The migrant balmiki community complains that regularised MCH employment—with the benefits of pension and assurance of intra-generational employment in the initial stages—consciously benefited the local madigas more than the methars. Madigas, however claim that the methars did not opt for *baldia*[11] or MCH employment as the payment here initially was just Rs 5 to Rs 7 per month. "Each methar family (sharing a common kitchen) serviced at least 200–300 dry latrines and earned much more than what was paid through the MCH."

Baneer Singh and the other men who worked as manual scavengers are reluctant to talk about their experiences. "What is there to talk about? It is not something to be proud of. It is worth forgetting those days."[12] He is more keen to announce that he managed to retire as an MCH staff and that one of his sons is an officer in the revenue department. The urge to climb the social ladder is strong. "We worked hard. Even after I got a full-time government job, I continued to service houses working day and night, so that I could secure a better life for my thirteen children."

Sixty-five-year-old Chandro, who came to Hyderabad from Haryana after marriage, is stoic. "Everyone has to do what is destined. When I got married, I was also provided a broom and a bucket along with my husband. At home, I had never done this cleaning job, but I knew I had little choice here." Like in other communities, patriarchy is strong. The balmikis do not allow their daughters to perform manual scavenging. "Once they wed, they become the property of their husband's families, who decide for them. While they are home, we make sure we don't allow them to do this work." The attitude is common across the states.

The segregation of women and men among safai karamcharis is as prevalent as it is in any other occupation, such as agriculture. Women, by and large, are the ones who manually clean the dry toilets, and heap the faeces into the bucket or trough outside the dry toilet. The men haul this away, either on a tractor or a handcart or rickshaw to the fields outside the town or village, and dump it there. As far as jobs and salaries go, there's no gender discrimination— both either get or do not get jobs (this depends on networking), and get the same wage. Men, of course, have far more mobility in acquiring the newer jobs (such as the *maistri* or overseer). Where rehabilitation is concerned, though women do the larger part of scavenging, they account for only 45 percent of those rehabilitated by APSCCFC, where they should have been 80 percent.

---

1 *Report of the AP Mission for Eradication of Manual Scavenging* (Hyderabad: AP Mission for Eradication of Manual Scavenging, 2001) 13.
2 Joint survey by the AP Scheduled Caste Cooperative Finance Corporation, and the Safai Karamchari Andolan, 2001.
3 Appendix 2 provides a district-wise break-up of dry toilets in Andhra Pradesh.
4 Safai karamcharis must necessarily internalise the ethos of scavenging to survive, if only in spirit. Wilson says that when he meets safai karamcharis in any town and asks them what they do, they reply '*mana pani chestunnamu*' ('we are doing *our* work'). He points out that no one refers to British imperialism as 'our' British rule, though the British ruled India for more than 300 years. Hence he stresses the necessity for the community to unlearn this internalisation, and for activists to sensitise the community that '*this is not our shit, it is their shit; it is not our work, it is their work that we are doing*'.
5 A prospective beneficiary of a government scheme has to present, along with identifying and qualifying papers, a demand draft for Rs 250 in favour of the local body.
6 We are told that the CDLs in Kurnool town are cleaned by halalkhors who are in turn paid by the permanent employees of the corporation.
7 Byreddi Rajashekhar Reddi, a powerful TDP faction leader of the area.
8 Interview with the author, 22 August 2004.
9 Suvvada Srinivas, "Coping with Degrading Work."
10 Author interview with balmiki elders Umed Singh and Anil Kumar, September 2004.
11 Baldia is Urdu for municipality.
12 Baneer Singh retired from the MCH over six years ago. Besides what his MCH job entailed, he was also cleaning latrines in private houses. He stopped both, but his wife continues to do the work.

7

Bezwada Wilson: Shepherd of the Manual Scavengers

Any account of manual scavenging in Andhra Pradesh is incomplete without the extraordinary story of Bezwada Wilson. The 38-year-old is the unquestioned leader of the Safai Karamchari Andolan. D. Babulal, an SKA activist from Kolar, says of Wilson: "When I think of Wilson working day and night for our people, I know that he should be called the Ambedkar of safai karamcharis." This section is based on discussions with Wilson over a period of time.

Wilson sports metal-rimmed spectacles and a thin beard. An earnest voice gives him the mild visage of a kindly priest. He does not possess a watch, and for everybody other than scavengers, he hardly spares any time.

Wilson was born into a madiga family in the Kolar Gold Fields (KGF), Karnataka. The madiga community in Kolar, almost entirely, was employed in dry latrine scavenging, or employed on the rolls as sanitary workers. It is Kolar with its 236 community dry toilets that probably shaped Wilson and his thinking. Established in 1870 by the British, Kolar, though in Karnataka, is dominated by a large percentage of a Tamil dalit workforce. In the 1960s and 1970s, with 76,000 workers, the KGF township had the single largest industrial workforce in India.[1] Given the risky nature of work in the mines, the workers largely tend to be dalits. In 1902, Kolar was also one of the first places in Asia to be electrified. The British did not electrify Delhi, their political capital, or Bombay, their commercial capital, but Kolar where their gold mines lay. Electrification was a priority in Kolar, given the profits that accrued to the empire from it. Public sanitation was not a priority since there was a mass of untouchables who could easily be pushed into the dirty work.

By the time Wilson was born in 1966, the Kolar township had a population of about two lakh. Sanitation in the town was a saga of neglect. There were no individual toilets; instead, the British devised large CDLs for the workers. These were serviced by manual scavengers, all of them were from Andhra, like Wilson's family. There were 236 CDLs with 1,500 seats in all. These were serviced by 236 manual scavengers—one for each CDL. Of these, 108 were permanent employees of KGF. The scavengers in Kolar did not use just baskets; they needed buckets to empty the shit into large bins; these bins were then emptied into tractors and taken to a dump on the outskirts. Wilson recalls that KGF derived considerable income by selling the dried excreta as fertilizer to farmers.

There was often tension between the Tamil and Telugu workers, the latter being addressed as thotti in a derogatory fashion, but Wilson doesn't recall being aware of untouchability. Yet the constant teasing by Tamil children in school made the young Wilson wish that his community would change its profession.

Wilson's family played a crucial role in his development. He was the youngest son, his eldest brother being twenty years older than him. He was therefore a much loved and protected child; he recalls being breast-fed even when he was in school. His mother, Rachel Bezwada, being a homemaker, also paid a lot of attention to Wilson. His alphabet learning came with reading the Bible when he was five years old. His mother's one wish was that her youngest son should become a pastor.

Wilson's family was also unique in that his father never beat Wilson's mother, unlike most men in the community. Wilson's father joined KGF as a permanent employee in 1935. Sent on a scavenging round, he came home to retch, and refused to do the work again.

He must have had a compassionate superior, because he never had to scavenge again and did gardening work. Wilson's eldest brother worked in the Indian Railways for four years. He then joined KGF. Both at the railways and KGF he was a sanitary worker—there was not much choice for the youth of this community. As soon as they applied for a job and filled the caste column, they were directed to scavenging irrespective of their qualification. Wilson recalls that when he passed his intermediate exams and applied at the local employment exchange, he too was directed to this occupation. His second brother escaped the dragnet by standing his ground and insisting that he would rather work in the mines.

Wilson had his upper primary education at Kuppam, Andhra Pradesh, staying in the SC hostel; his later studies were at Kolar and Hyderabad. He completed his postgraduate degree in Political Science in Bangalore University and joined the Bachelor of Divinity course in the United Theosophical College, Bangalore. Besides his mother's urging, Wilson's move towards a vocation in the church stemmed from his belief that his community, a deeply religious people, would accept change and reform if they were initiated through the church.[2] Since 1982, he was involved with various church-based social activities—Sunday schools for children, road-cleaning campaigns, tree-planting, adult education and deaddiction from alcoholism, then a rampant problem among the workers at KGF. He saw that children studied up to the sixth or seventh class, then dropped out if they failed. They did not have to look far for employment. If they went to KGF, they were immediately recruited as manual scavengers, or in a sanitised form, as sanitary workers. Wilson thought that if he could push children through the tenth class, and later into a vocational course, they could take up other professions and escape scavenging.

Wilson's work with deaddiction pushed him once again into work on scavenging. All the addicts told him that they drank because they had to—the work forced them. Wilson became curious: what was the work like? This is not say that he was completely unaware of it. The excreta from the toilets was every day scooped into large bins placed just outside the toilet, if not in full public view, at least accessible to the interested viewer. He says it is like looking at a photograph, being temporarily shocked, and then moving on. If one experienced the real thing, it would remain in memory forever. Wilson wanted to know, wanted to share the experience of his community's workers. When he asked them if he could come along, they wouldn't let him. They would give him a cup of tea and fob him off. But Wilson did not let go easily, and finally he saw what they were doing. This was in 1989.

One man in the group was trying to manually empty out the contents of the excreta bin at the dry toilet. As the tractor to haul out the excreta arrives only once in two days, the faeces is cleaned every day and dumped into the bin. The man was trying to break the surface of the hardened excreta in the bin by hitting it with his bucket, when the bucket was pulled into the seething, soft mass inside. Not wanting to lose his bucket, the worker plunged his arm to lift the bucket, and tried to clean his soiled right arm with his clean left. In a flash, Wilson saw this, and recalls how he flung away the bucket, and shouted and wept like a mad man.

"I lay on the ground by the side of the pit, and wept. I had no answers to the sight I saw, I wanted to die. I wept continuously. Earlier, I was the one to pester the workers; now the roles were reversed. They were upset and asked me continually what the matter was. What had happened? Why was I weeping? Their questions saddened me even more. What had happened? After what I had seen, the world had turned upside down for me. I said I wanted to die, and that they should stop doing this work. I think my grief affected them. For the first time, they admitted that they too found the work repulsive. But what could they do? They would be dismissed if they refused, and there were mouths to feed at home."

Later, Wilson reconciled himself to the only stand that he could possibly take. "I couldn't eat, I couldn't sleep. I had only two options: either I had to die, or I had to work to stop the practice. The first was easy, the second difficult. I told myself that I would not achieve anything by dying." Supported by his family, he announced to his people: "This is my personal problem now: I will do a dharna before the KGF head office. If you want to support me, do it. If you don't, I will anyway go ahead."

What had been festering within Wilson for several years now broke forth, and he decided for himself that he would not allow his brother to work at scavenging; he would not allow his cousins; he would not allow anyone. He understood that the major problem with his community did not lie in alcoholism, poverty, unemployment or illiteracy, but in the forced work of cleaning other people's excreta. Consequently, Wilson's and the SKA's stand on manual scavenging has been uncompromising—the total abolition of manual scavenging. Various organisations and government committees have called for 'rehabilitation' of scavengers, and 'amelioration' of their conditions; Gandhi had asked for giving the profession 'nobility'; however, the SKA demands nothing short of abolition of dry toilets. It understands that a single dry toilet anywhere in India, given the nature of the caste system, will instantly create a caste of manual scavengers.

Trade unions and even some dalit groups have demanded that the SKA organise manual scavengers into a union. Wilson sees no merit in this view. "Why should we organise them? To demand better wages and living conditions? I am criticised for being anti-institution, anti-organisation. But our strength does not grow with a powerful organisation of manual scavengers. We can only be powerful when there are no manual scavengers." According to Wilson, the SKA's primary mandate is to abolish manual scavenging, not perpetuate it with a strong organisation.

He understands, however, that the abolition has to be done primarily by groups of manual scavengers themselves in the absence of political will and the apathy of civil society. For Wilson to have arrived at this understanding required a rare sensitivity and native intelligence. Notably, the KGF constituency elected communist party MLAS for twenty years.[3] KGF workers formed the base of the Left parties among industries in south India. When KGF was declared a reserved constituency in 1962, the nominee of a faction of the Republican Party of India was elected for three terms. Both the CPI(M) and the RPI are avowedly pro-poor, and both have close linkages with dalits and a history of sustained mass work. Yet they were indifferent in perceiving and interpreting peoples' problems; both ignored the role of scavenging in the dehumanisation of an entire community.

In May 1982, Wilson attempted to work through the church, because he himself is deeply religious, and because he knows that people of his community will flock to the church as to no other organisation.[4] He says wryly, "The church does not accept scavenging theology. The church and its ministers want to talk of the kingdom hereafter, but not about the living hell today." While there were priests who even refused to pray for manual scavengers because they were doing 'dirty work', Wilson recalls the encouragement from other priests who felt that the abolition of manual scavenging was noble work.

In 1986–87, Wilson first called representatives of the thirteen colonies of safai karamcharis[5] in Kolar for a meeting to discuss ending the practice; the safai karamcharis refused to support him. Their reaction was: 'You fool! All these years we have been carrying shit without anyone knowing about it. Now if we discuss the problem openly, everyone will get to know about it.' He continued on his lonely mission looking out for allies. He participated in a cycle rally in 1991 from Chittoor to Hyderabad with NGOs and dalit groups.[6] Slowly, his solitary campaign picked up momentum. He wrote unacknowledged letters to the KGF officialdom seeking an end to the practice of manual scavenging; in 1991, he wrote to the chief minister of Karnataka, and the prime minister; he got his friends to write letters to newspapers; in the same year, he published a pamphlet describing the practice and condemning it.[7] When the central government enacted an Act of parliament in 1993 banning manual scavenging, it seemed to Wilson a vindication of his efforts.[8]

Following this, he sent a letter with photographs of dry toilets to P.A.K. Shettigar, then managing director of KGF, threatening action under the law if dry latrines continued in the KGF township. This letter was acknowledged; the system was finally responding. Wilson was even offered money to withdraw his campaign.[9] His real break came in 1994, when the Bangalore-based daily *Deccan Herald* published a report on the dry latrines in the Kolar Gold Fields.[10] Questions were raised in parliament, and a spate of Karnataka ministers and MLAS descended on Wilson's house in Kolar to make political capital.[11] In an emergency board meeting on 16 April 1994, KGF decided to convert all dry toilets to waterborne ones, and transfer all manual scavengers to non-scavenging occupations.

When work on conversion of latrines and rehabilitation really began in Kolar in 1994,[12] Wilson had become a hero. Characteristically, he decided to leave Kolar before the halo became unmanageable. He worked for two years with the YMCA in Bangalore as its regional coordinator, with a mandate to organise manual scavengers in Karnataka. He toured the length and breadth of the state in search of manual scavengers.[13] His contact with dalit organisations in Andhra Pradesh—the state with the largest number of dry toilets in the south—deepened, and he decided to shift his focus here in 1996 when he was repeatedly invited by Paul Divakar, then associated with Prajwala, an NGO in Chittoor district, Andhra Pradesh. He found a friend, philosopher and guide in S.R. Sankaran, a retired IAS officer known for his ability to bend the administration towards the needs of the poor, particularly dalits and adivasis.

---

1 In 1980, there was a reduction of about 12,000–13,000 in the workforce.
2 All the manual scavengers in Kuppam were Christian.
3 For twenty years, CPI's Vajravel Chetti, and CPI(M)'s S. Rajagopal (who defected to the Congress after election) and T.S. Mani were elected from Kolar. C.M. Arumugam from the RPI also represented Kolar.
4 About 60 percent of the manual scavengers in Kolar are Christians, largely of the Church of South India denomination. There are three

churches in Kolar served by one priest. Of the three priests who have served there in the past three decades, only one is from the safai karamchari community, the other two have been of caste-Hindu origin.

5   Of the thirteen colonies, five were large with about hundred houses each; the other eight were small with about thirty to fifty houses. The safai karamcharis accounted for a thousand houses in all with a population of 5,000.

6   The rally was organised by the newly formed Andhra Pradesh Vyavasaya Coolie Sangham to celebrate the Ambedkar centenary year.

7   The pamphlet, in Telugu, was titled, 'Malam mose paddadhitiki vyatirekanga udhyamiddam'(Let us rise against the practice of carrying shit).

8   The Act was not passed because of compunctions about manual scavenging. It was passed because of international norms on urban sanitation. The Ministry of Urban Development spearheaded the Act.

9   It was I.D.P. Salappa—ironically of the Salappa Committee which in 1972 submitted the 'Karnataka Report of the Committee on Improvement of Living and Working Conditions of Sweepers and Scavengers'—who offered him money. KGF authorities also suggested to Wilson that he could take a loan of Rs.1 lakh from them and start a printing press. The MLAs who visited Wilson's house in KGF included then labour minister C. Gurunath of the Janata Dal, social welfare minister Ramesh Jigijunagi and Babu Heddur Shetti, Janta Dal state vice-president.

10 See Prasanna Kumar, "Shame," *Deccan Herald*, 15 April 1994.

11 This was in the context of a Congress government at the centre with the Janata Dal ruling in Karnataka. KGF being a central government institution in Karnataka, it made good politics for state leaders to raise a hue and cry.

12 The permanent safai karamcharis were transferred to workshops in minor technical posts, while the temporary workers were rehabilitated in different ways: fourteen were given autorickshaws, five were given ration shop dealerships, three kerosene shop dealerships, and the rest were absorbed as sweepers in KGF.

13 Wilson associated himself with groups like the Dalit Sangharsha Samiti, but they were not aware of the practice though several dry latrines existed in Karnataka. He recalls that they did not even come close to acknowledging the truth of it (unlike dalits in Andhra Pradesh).

8
Safai Karamchari Andolan

The Safai Karamchari Andolan, in its own words, "was born out of the anguish and the anger of a few members from within the community. It was started in 1996 in Vijayawada by a few human rights activists with an objective to liberate and rehabilitate manual scavengers from their caste-based hereditary and inhuman occupation."[1] The three people intimately connected with it since inception are Bezwada Wilson, S.R. Sankaran and Paul Divakar, currently a senior leader of the National Campaign for Dalit Human Rights (NCDHR) based in Hyderabad. The SKA is unregistered. In 1997 it conducted a preliminary survey in the municipalities of twelve districts—Chittoor, Anantapur, Kurnool, Cuddapah, Nellore, Ongole, Mehboobnagar, East Godavari, West Godavari, Guntur, Krishna, Visakhapatnam—to arrive at an understanding of the issue. This survey revealed that of the 109 municipalities in twelve districts, forty-three employed dalits for manual scavenging. The other municipalities surveyed were scavenging-free.

Today, the SKA has eight members as its core team in Andhra Pradesh. They are Pennobilesu from Anantapur, Saraswati from Nizamabad, Sreedevi from West Godavari, Swarnalatha and Appa Rao from East Godavari, Roshan Babu from Prakasham and Kamal Kumar from Kurnool. All the core team members are from local scavenging communities. The SKA's national core team comprises Deepthi Sukumar from Chennai, K. Anuradha from Hyderabad and Rev Dr Y. Moses from Bangalore. The national board formed in

2000 has a fourteen-member campaign coordination committee with two safai karamcharis each from Rajasthan, Mumbai and Uttar Pradesh.

When the SKA started its work, the activists faced difficulties as the safai karamcharis wondered what alternative work they would find. Other fraternal organisations suggested that the emphasis should instead be on better monetary benefits and entitlements. Wilson recalls facing a dilemma at several moments in the struggle—whether the SKA's position that manual scavenging should be abolished and rooted out without any preconditions was right. The SKA activists suggested to the safai karamcharis that other members of the dalit community were not doing too well either and were in fact struggling for a livelihood. The safai karamcharis, too, could join the struggles of the rest of the dalits and give up a life where even if monetary benefits were enhanced, indignity of labour would persist. Wilson recalls assuming a non-antagonistic attitude to all questions, and trying hard to convince people. He found it hard to convince his own people that if they had to move forward, they had to leave the work. 'Will you feed us?' they sometimes asked. He would ask whether they wanted their sons and daughters to continue in the profession. 'No.' He would then counter: 'I am your son too. Tell me whether you should continue in the profession.'

The SKA has been lobbying since 1997 at different levels—the village, district, state and national capital—to influence the government and other stakeholders (such as the railways, military establishments, heavy industries and factories) to implement the Employment of Manual Scavengers and Construction of Dry Latrines (Prohibition) Act, penalise people violating the Act, initiate measures to demolish dry latrines, and rehabilitate the scavengers. It has also been pursuing the matter with the chairman of the National Commission for Safai Karamcharis. Simply put, the objective of the SKA is to abolish all dry toilets.

The surveys and resurveys conducted by the SKA over the years were arduous since they had to battle indifference and denial by the state administration. Initially, a simple pilot survey in ten municipalities was taken up in 1996. The then social welfare minister Kadiam Srihari denied the veracity of the report when they presented him the findings the same year. About this time, Bezwada Wilson took nearly a hundred photographs of different toilets and sent them with details of the place and the name of scavenger to the social welfare minister, the managing director of APSCCFC, the chief minister and the NHRC. While the NHRC took the letter and photographs on file and forwarded them to the chief secretary of the Andhra Pradesh government for action, the MD of APSCCFC invited the SKA group for a discussion. Soon, several media reports appeared on manual scavenging in the state, particularly in Anantapur district. The government was worried by the media attention. The 400-seater CDL in Anantapur—photographs of which had been used by the media— was demolished soon after, and the scavenger, Narayanamma,[2] was rehabilitated in an alternative employment by the district collector. The MD of APSCCFC now formally asked the SKA to undertake a survey— funded by the corporation—of all dry toilets in the state. This survey was undertaken in April–May 2001 with 240 enumerators. During this survey, Wilson photographed every CDL he saw. First, the immediate surroundings of the toilet were shot to dispel any doubt about its location; then the inside of the toilet was documented in graphic detail; and a third photograph showed the worker (usually a woman) cleaning. Wilson recalls the first photograph he took in his life, which was aired in 1995 on the show *60 Minutes* on the American television channel CBS. The photographs and the work testify to an immense labour of love, for no professional could have gone around thousands of CDLs and continued to shoot with any clarity of vision.

All the enumerators in the survey were dalits, and about half of them were from the scavenging castes. Keeping in view the earlier disbelief of the authorities, the survey questionnaire was prepared carefully. (The four-page colour folders, including colour photographs—sampled as a frontispiece in this book—give an idea of the results of the survey for every CDL.) There were two orientation sessions—one for the enumerators and the other for the executive directors of APSCCFC from all districts. Every town and major panchayat in the twenty-three districts of the state was covered, with the APSCCFC paying the enumerators Rs 300 per municipality and Rs 100 per gram panchayat, the total budget being Rs 2.35 lakh.

The survey report was submitted both to the MD and the various executive directors in September 2001. When these results were shown to the Department of Municipal Administration for initiating action, they refused to accept them as authentic and denied the existence of most toilets. A second exercise was then undertaken in 2002 to videograph each CDL—a three-minute videograph of both the scavenging and the visits by users. Here again, APSCCFC paid for the videography and the SKA activists arranged to show the toilets to the videographers. Still photographs were also sought and these were taken by Wilson himself. In 2003, the executive director of APSCCFC, Kurnool district, claimed that he had demolished/converted all the CDLS. The SKA was therefore asked to redo the survey. A complete resurvey of Kurnool district was done by the SKA in 2003, and it was proved that the executive director had misrepresented facts. The SKA was now asked to do a complete resurvey, but they refused. They felt that they were spending all their time and resources in survey after survey with no change in the ground reality.

The SKA had filed a writ petition in the Supreme Court in 2003 in the belief that the apex court would be able to give clear and time-bound directions.[3] Nothing happened. The SKA addressed a letter to all district collectors, gram panchayat secretaries and municipal commissioners on 29 May 2004, drawing their attention to the provisions of the Employment of Manual Scavengers and Construction of Dry Latrines (Prohibition) Act, 1993, and the AP Mission's plan to demolish all dry latrines by December 2002. The letter also informed that in case those dry latrines under the jurisdiction of these officers were not demolished forthwith, the SKA would be doing so in July–August 2004.

On 17 July, the SKA began its 'physical demolition' campaign in Kakinada. The SKA demolition squad passed from town to town. Theirs was a peculiar job. They were demolishing illegal structures, but the demolitions were outside the pale of law. Their actions were extra-legal as illustrated by the incident in the munsiff court at Yellareddy (described in the next chapter). The statutes of parliament may declare an institution illegal, but no citizen or group can abolish the illegal institution; only a statutory body can.

---

1 Minutes of the first meeting held in Vijayawada on 8 August 1996.
2 Featured on the cover of this book.
3 The petitioners sought enforcement of their fundamental right guaranteed under Article 17 (right against untouchability) read with Articles 14, 19 and 21 guaranteeing equality, freedom, and protection of life and personal liberty respectively. They urged the Supreme Court to issue time-bound directions to the Union of India and the various states to take effective steps for the elimination of manual scavenging simultaneously with the formulation and implementation of comprehensive plans for rehabilitation of all persons employed as manual scavengers. During the recent hearing of the case on 29 April 2005, a bench consisting of Justices S.N. Variava and H.K. Sema issued an interim order directing that every department/ministry of the union government and each of the state governments should, within six months, file an affidavit through a senior officer who would take personal responsibility for verifying the facts stated in the affidavit. If the affidavit admits the existence of manual scavenging in the particular department, or public sector undertaking or corporation, then it should indicate a time-bound programme within which targets for liberation and rehabilitation of manual scavengers and their ultimate eradication is proposed to be achieved. The court warned the governments against making false statements in these affidavits. See "A Case for Human Dignity," *Frontline*, 17 June 2005.

9

The Struggle for Self-Respect

The demolition campaign was planned along with solidarity groups, particularly dalit groups, who participated extensively in the Telangana districts of Adilabad, Karimnagar, Nizamabad, Warangal, Khammam, Rangareddy, Mehboobnagar and Medak. In Kakinada and Hyderabad, groups affiliated to the CPI(M), such as All India Democratic Women's Association and Jana Vignana Vedika, also participated. In each place, the campaign was coordinated by the eight-member SKA state core group. There was another team that visited all the areas slated for the rally/demolition a day or two ahead of the main team. The recce team prepared the ground for the main team by distributing pamphlets and meeting the various stakeholders—safai karamcharis, users, gram panchayat/municipality officials, local dalit groups and other peoples' organisations—to explain the objectives of the rally and ask for support. Where they expected the situation to be possibly tense, they sought protection from the local police station. They also pasted campaign posters at strategic points in the town/village. Blue SKA ribbons and badges were also given to the local organisers who would plan the logistics of the movement of the procession, the community lunch for the day, and the tools—pickaxes, shovels and crowbars—for the actual demolition. The recce team also informed the local print and television media about the programme a day ahead.

Along with local safai karamcharis and solidarity groups, a crowd of at least a hundred was gathered. The campaign usually began with the garlanding of the statue of Dr B.R. Ambedkar at the venue, a procession around the town, a visit to the local gram panchayat or municipality where there was a demonstration (and an informal discussion with local officials, elected representatives, and often, the local police), and finally a march to the local community dry latrine. Here, to the accompaniment of slogans, the structure was razed to the ground with crowbars and pickaxes. Following the demolition and prior to it, discussions were held with the users, rounded off by a community lunch arranged by the local scavenging community. Where there was no demolition, there were extensive meetings with the local safai karamcharis. In most places, the local district-level media, both print and electronic, covered the event.

Kakinada, 17 July 2004

The campaign began on 17 July 2004—the twentieth anniversary of the Karamchedu carnage—in Kakinada, a coastal town and the headquarters of East Godavari district. Kakinada, one of the richest towns in the state, has a rich and fertile hinterland watered by the Godavari river. It boasts of a harbour, has a well-developed fishing industry, and has struck oil recently. The district also houses 1,200 dry toilets which are cleaned manually by safai karamcharis. The first demolition of a CDL passed without incident; the only hint of opposition came from the municipal authorities who wanted to know whether the rallyists had permission from the government. Brushing aside the need for permission to demolish, the rallyists asked them whether the municipality had an explanation for why the toilets were still around after the ban on manual scavenging was effected in 1993. SKA core team member Saraswati recalls that it was raining continuously in Kakinada on the day of the demolition, but no one left the rally. On 18 July, there were demolitions in Kaikaram, West Godavari district. On 19 July, in Machilipatnam, the headquarters of Krishna district, another rich district in the state, a dry toilet in Ogis Pet was demolished. On 20 July, the demolition campaign moved to Gadi Veedhi, Kasimpeta, Visakhapatnam. On 21 July, the dry toilet in Kaketi Veedhi, Vizianagaram district headquarters, was demolished.

The slogans of the safai karamcharis mingled with the dust raised by the demolitions:

Maaku rendu chetule, meeku rendu chetule (You have two hands, we have two hands)

Puttuka kaadu, karma kaadu, safai ma pani kaadu (Not by birth, not by karma, scavenging is not our job)

Swatantra bharatamlo paki pani—siggu-siggu (Scavenging work in Independent India—Shame, Shame)

Cheyyi cheyyi kalupudam, dry latrinelanu koolchudam (Let us join hands and demolish the dry latrines)

During the drive, the SKA issued daily bulletins. One such report said: "After four days of travelling around four districts, and meetings and discussions with the community and persons working in these dry toilets, we are convinced that even members who are earning their livelihood through manual scavenging are keen to give up this work and take up other livelihood. The presence of community dry latrines and its use by civil society in a way force the safai karamcharis to continue in this occupation. They have also in some cases mindlessly, in some cases owing to tradition, and in some cases out of pressure continued to carry on this task. However, if the dry toilets were not there, the problems of the safai karamcharis would not have continued to this day."

The second phase of the demolition drive, devoted to the four Rayalaseema districts, began in Chittoor on 5 August 2004. The SKA team was shocked to discover that some educated professionals, including a lawyer, continued to have dry toilets in their homes. Since there were no CDLS in Chittoor district, there were no demolitions here. On 6 August, the team proceeded to Cuddapah—present chief minister Y.S. Rajashekhar Reddy's native district—and demolished a dry toilet in Ravindra Nagar. The team then moved to

Kallur village in Garladinne mandal, 20 km from Anantapur town, where the CDL near the gram panchayat office, in the centre of the village, was demolished on 7 August. A few months ago when government officials, led by the executive officer, went to demolish this CDL, they had been badly beaten up by the users. The users of this toilet questioned the SKA team but the matter was settled soon.[1] On 8 August, the sixty-seater CDL at Pathabanda Street, Nandikotkur, Kurnool district, was demolished.

For the third phase, the team covered the Telangana districts. On 9 August, the team demolished the CDL at Kindiger, Narayanpet mandal, Mehboobnagar district. On 11 August, the team moved to Ibrahimpatnam in Ranga Reddy district, where they inspected twenty individual dry toilets in houses.

On 15 August, the SKA team moved to Adilabad. Since there are twenty individual dry latrines but no CDLs there was no demolition. The next stops were at Godavarikhani, Warangal and Khammam. In all these places, there were no dry latrines, but the SKA team met the community of methars and discussed their problems. Even where there are no dry latrines, the community faces grave problems of livelihood which all assets-less dalits face, added to the fact that safai karamcharis are largely migrant communities—methars in Telangana; rellis in East Godavari, West Godavari and Krishna districts; yanadis in Prakasam and Guntur districts; and the migrant madigas in Rayalaseema. Migrant communities have less of a voice, little networking and are usually tainted by their past occupation. Even when they quit manual scavenging, society summons them for any dirty, menial work.

Yellareddy, 16 August 2004

On 16 August, the SKA team descended on Yellareddy, Nizamabad district, which has twelve IDLs and two CDLs. One of the CDLs, an eight-seater, is on the premises of a junior civil court judge and was being used by the court staff till March 2005. Vinod Gokalkar, 35, used to clean all the latrines in the town. The court paid him Rs 750 per month for cleaning the CDL on the court premises, and he earned another Rs 1,000 by cleaning all the IDLS. As the rallyists were demolishing the CDL—with Vinod striking the first blow—the court authorities stopped them, saying that they could not demolish the latrine without permission. They presented the SKA team with an order signed by the chief ministerial officer of the junior civil judge's court, which said:

> There are two dry latrines in the premises of the Junior Civil Judge's Court, Yellareddy. Today i.e. on 16-8-04, the safai karamchari volunteers have come to demolish the same. In order to protect of the property of the court they are prevented from demolishing the same till the necessary permission is obtained from the Hon'ble District Judge, Nizamabad.

The rallyists made a representation to the mandal revenue officer and the local sub-inspector of police. The SI initially refused to take the complaint saying he did not know about the Act, and that since the processionists were creating public nuisance, they could be arrested.

Vinod, his wife and two school-going daughters, comprised the only scavenger family in the town. They are methars, originally from Haryana, who migrated about four generations ago, according to Vinod. His close relatives are in Kamareddy and Nizamabad, towns close by. Vinod was threatened with a show-cause notice for talking to the SKA activists and to reporters of a TV channel who covered the event two days later. Soon, he left the job at the court because they stopped paying him. He now works with the SKA in Hyderabad.

Wherever the SKA went, municipality and gram panchayat officials denied the very existence of dry latrines in their jurisdiction. Sometimes, officials—civic body authorities, gram panchayat functionaries, revenue and police officials, including the district superintendent of police—had no idea that there was an Act banning manual scavenging. In places such as Chirala, Nandikotkur, Machilipatnam and Kasimkota, poorer people were using CDLS, though the SKA activists found that in Narasapuram, Anakapalle,

Kakinada, Ravulapalem and Anaparthi in East Godavari and West Godavari districts, people owning property worth Rs 15 lakhs were also using CDLS.

Chirala, 31 August 2004

In thirty minutes, the dry toilet in Vittalnagar was razed to the ground by about a hundred activists of the Safai Karamchari Andolan. Kamaragiri Kotamma, a safai karamchari, delivered the first blow with an iron rod. Amidst cries of *ailesso aiso!* the 15 x 15 ft dry toilet constructed about twenty years ago by the Chirala municipality came crashing down, leaving behind only raised platforms as mute testimony to the days when it was the duty of one set of people to manually clean other peoples' excrement.

Earlier in the day, the activists gathered at the Ambedkar statue near the railway station, garlanded it, and proceeded to the municipal office where they had a heated discussion with the chairperson and the office manager who denied the existence of any dry toilet and then advised the activists not to demolish the 'nonexistent' toilets. Wilson waved evidence of one CDL at Vittalnagar, thirty-five dry latrines in the Chirala division, and seven in the Chirala municipality. "If you find it so difficult to even listen to us, how much more difficult would it be for our people to clean your shit!"

The dry toilets did exist, and there were fifteen droppings. At Vittalnagar, when the activists began demolishing the CDL, the users stood around with sullen faces. But when the users realised that the demolition squad comprised safai karamcharis themselves, the rumbles of protest died down. The rally culminated in a meeting at Vijayanagar, Chirala, where the victims of the Karamchedu carnage now live.

The culmination of the two-month blitzkrieg was a rally in Hyderabad on 16 September 2004 preceded by a procession. Hundreds of manual scavengers from all over the state marched in the procession. (Many towns in Andhra Pradesh would have remained dirty that day.) Narayanamma from Chirala had come despite her father being seriously ill. After she reached Hyderabad, she was informed that he had died and the funeral would be held that day. But she refused to return, saying, "I cannot miss this first ever meeting of my people." A significant feature of the meeting was the participation of women from the methar community in the Old City. Sheetal spoke boldly: "We belong to the same community, you and I. We must leave this work (scavenging), you and I. I am educated, and I have dreams for us. Join us, all of you."

The rally changed the perceptions of several SKA activists. Kamal Kumar said, "I had earlier thought that there were dry latrines only in Kurnool district where I live and work. When I went around the state, I was happy to see my safai karamchari brethren everywhere, but also sad that they were still doing this work." Among those present was Rajashekhar, who has an M.A. in Political Science, and works as a sweeper and manual scavenger in Razole of East Godavari district. D. Babulal from SKA, Kolar, said: "For the first time in my life, I spoke to governmental authorities in Kaikaram in a decided fashion. I was afraid initially, but picked up courage because my team was present. We demanded that the authorities help in demolishing the CDL there." Roshan Babu, from Prakasam district, a member of the SKA core team, said: "I was initially afraid when I had to speak to the municipal authorities. There are twelve CDLs in Kasimkota, and I was deputed in the team that called on the executive officer of the gram panchayat. When I asked him to cooperate in the demolition of only one CDL, he refused. He also said that we should not demolish it. He asked us for a month's time. I was filled with sudden anger and raged at him, 'You want my people to clean shit for another month! We will not tolerate this. We will demolish it immediately.' We left the gram panchayat office to demolish the CDL."

Reactions from users and authorities

Users in most cases are the poorer sections of society. The richer sections have private toilets. However, in East Godavari and West Godavari districts, even the rich were using dry toilets. Activists recall that the opposition to demolitions was largely verbal, but hurtful nevertheless. "We pay money, do the *pakivallu* do it for free? If they (the scavengers) don't do this, what else are they going to do—run our shops?"

The users in Chirala were angry when there were suggestions that they could apply for individual sanitary latrines (ISLS) from the municipality. "They make us roam a hundred times, but will not sanction it, unless we pay hefty bribes," they said. They showed the SKA team ten ISLS with no walls and roofs, where the hole was dug, but the seat had not been installed.

The executive officer of the Nandikotkur gram panchayat recalls that when the issue of a ban on manual scavenging was placed on the agenda, and when he explained the penal provisions, there was absolute silence. After the meeting of panchayat ward members, the elected representatives commented that stopping manual scavenging was simply impossible. The users—who accounted for thousands of votes—were incensed, and were pressuring the ward members saying they would use their voting right to settle scores with them.[2] The scavengers, who serviced the sixteen CDLS, were only a handful. In the eight days of bedlam that followed the strike by the permanent employees who refused to clean the CDLS, there were repeated dharnas by the users (one led by the CPI-ML New Democracy faction) and the gram panchayat had to lock its offices to protect itself. Fear of cholera spread, and the women discovered worms and insects in the CDLS that they continued to use. The blame game among politicians resulted in the Telugu Desam Party (TDP) cadre spreading the rumour that the new Congress government (which has completed one hundred days in power) had banned dry toilets. Congress workers were thus forced to take a more 'radical' stand. They encouraged women from the user communities to besiege the gram panchayat office, the latter being under TDP control. Someone organised ten women from each locality and took them in lorries to Kurnool, where they met the collector, Ajay Jain. He, in turn, is said to have promised to construct pour-flush toilets in two months. The MLA, Gouru Charita of the Congress, too visited some of the affected localities and promised action.

CPI activists in Nandikotkur, who are usually in the forefront of struggles against atrocities, were silent about the issue of manual scavenging. There was no response to the stand that manual scavenging cannot be condoned on any count. However, they would launch into a diatribe on how the Scheduled Castes have it good in every sphere. "Fifty out of seventy teachers in the Midthur mandal are SCs," the CPI activists retorted. "Only the well-off among the SCs grab reserved seats. They do not help their brethren. In a family of four, we find three are salaried employees. Is that fair?" they asked.

The CDL near Rajaveedhi Pata Masjid presented an extremely unpleasant sight. A rancid broad nala bubbling over with fetid odours passed under it, and the pathway was littered with refuse. An adolescent girl was squatting outside the toilet in full public view. Not far away, the gram panchayat had constructed a pay-and-use public toilet. The man in-charge collected half a rupee for urinals, and one rupee for defecation. There were separate wings for men and women. The outflow from this toilet was contributing considerably to the smell of the nala.

As soon as we reached the CDL, the users gathered around us clamouring that we see their houses. These were so small, they said, that there was no place to construct a toilet. Some houses had one room, some even three, and with some adjustment, toilets could certainly have been constructed within the houses, but they were clearly opposed to the construction of a toilet within the house. In their worldview, a toilet should only be outside.

"You people have big houses, so you can have toilets inside your homes. We have such small houses, and four times the people you have stay inside our homes. How can we make space for a toilet? Besides, it will spread germs inside our homes. We are people who work hard for a living. If we fall ill, how will we work?" There was a mob that gheraoed the SKA team. There were about forty to fifty users; most of the vociferous people were Muslim women.

The lane is called Metharolla Veedhi. *Metharolla* here refers to a 'backward' caste that works with bamboo. Varalakshmi lives in a one-roomed house with her husband, mother-in-law, and two sisters-in-law; they use the space outside, which is technically gram panchayat property, to stock their bamboo wares. Even their thatched bathroom is on the road. Her aunt next door has five daughters-in-law, all of them in one room. Over 200 people here use the CDL.

They were aghast when I suggested that they could use the pay-and-use toilet. "Why should we pay money to shit?" was one reaction, whereas some women felt that using a toilet that is on the main road, in full public view, was not appropriate. A suggestion they had for solving the problem was that holes be drilled into the toilet, so that the excreta passed directly into the nala below. The other was that pigs be allowed freely so that they ate the excreta. In the eight days of the strike, they had in fact removed the rocks that refused entry to the animals, and the pigs had done the rest. Clearly, the users were at their wits' end.

In the next CDL at Pinjarapet, not far from the Metharolla Veedhi in Nandikotkur, Muslim women working as agricultural labourers gathered around the SKA team. One woman asked aggressively: "Why should not the scavengers clean the toilets as before? They have been doing it for generations, they are used to the work." Where they were earlier living in villages, they didn't need any toilets, because there was enough space outside. In the town, women, especially young girls, had no place to go; and 'in times like these, it was simply not safe'. Kasim Bi was vehement: "A latrine is more important than food or water. We can starve for a day, but can we hold back excreta?"

The SKA drive of July–August 2004 had positive results in many places. In Kaikaram, for instance, where the SKA demolished one CDL, the gram panchayat demolished the other eleven. When the SKA staged a rally in Ongole, the fallout was in nearby Kanigiri where the gram panchayat demolished thirteen of the fourteen CDLS. In Yellareddy, where the recalcitrant court had given an order forbidding the demolition, the CDL was demolished in March 2005. West Godavari district now has a special officer—appointed in April 2005—to survey and commission the demolition of dry toilets. In other places, the district collectors/joint collectors have called for internal meetings with concerned officials to speed up the demolition of dry toilets.

---

1   Since the SKA activists had known of the earlier mauling of the executive officer, they went a day earlier to the police, apprised them of the day's agenda, and asked for protection. With this, the crowd of users was subdued.
2   The town, with a population of 39,584 according to the 2001 census, consists of backward castes, SCs and banias. The dominant caste is reddy.

10
A Community in Transition

All official literature on manual scavenging—especially committee reports—indicate that the manual scavengers, particularly the bhangis, hold a monopoly over their work and fiercely defend it from newer entrants. Indeed, there are even offensive suggestions that the scavengers do not consider their work dirty. The Barve Committee blames the victims.

> Ancestors of these Bhangis were just field labourers of a low caste, but never did the work of scavenging. Some of these people took to the dirty work of cleansing the latrines for the sake of profit. Slowly this developed into a monopoly. The stage was reached when the Bhangis wanted to exploit this monopoly and a sort of customary right was thus developed. By force of habit the Bhangi lost his self respect to such an extent that his did not consider the dirty work of cleansing latrines as a curse from which he should endeavour to extricate himself.[1]

The Malkani Committee (1965) has this to say on 'the customary rights of scavengers': "Scavenging has been a way of life for the family. A fatalistic attitude pervades the whole outlook due to the lack of education and the absence of other openings for employment."[2]

What is striking is the silence of the scavengers on an issue that concerns them. People who actually lift excreta are reserved in their description of the work, and it seemed incorrect to probe and press them further. However, the rapidity with which they joined the SKA and identified themselves with it foregrounds the intensity of their feelings, one presumes, about the work.³ For instance, Vinod Gokalkar, the scavenger at the munsiff court in Yellareddy, met the SKA group for the first time on 16 August 2004. When he realised that the SKA members were from his own community and when their objectives were explained to him, he struck the first blow on the CDL within half an hour. This was the toilet his family had been cleaning for two generations, and he for twenty years.

In Nandikotkur, the reaction was similar to Vinod's. The SKA group met the sweepers on the morning of 8 August 2004. Within an hour, the sweepers accompanied the team and demolished one CDL and refused to clean the others thereafter. The SKA team left Nandikotkur that night, and the sweepers were under tremendous pressure from the CDL users and the local administration to continue scavenging, but they steadfastly refused. Since they were permanent employees of the gram panchayat, the panchayat simply allotted other duties to them. The panchayat was forced to hire four new people—again, three madigas and one halalkhor—for the job.

One therefore needs to read into the silences of the community. Their silence foregrounds the inaction of the rest of society. The degree of alienation of the scavengers from their work is immense but has remained unexpressed, waiting for a moment of release. For the safai karamcharis of Andhra Pradesh, such a moment was facilitated by the SKA led by Bezwada Wilson.

The SKA has focused on manual scavenging in the dry toilets of Andhra Pradesh. But the fact is even if all the dry toilets were to be demolished, manual scavenging would continue in the cleaning of nalas, drains, community latrines, emptying pit latrines and septic tanks. Caste notions still define this work, and almost always madigas, yanadis and rellis are used for this work by both institutions and individuals. In the case of toilet and drainage cleaning undertaken privately, the controls and standards are even more difficult to establish. Picking up faeces, with little or no cover, and using dalits to do the job, constitutes an institutional form of untouchability that also needs to be tackled. The existing practices of sanitation in municipalities need to be reformed and upgraded so that no one—from any caste—has to pick up faeces manually. The SKA's stand has been one of complete opposition to picking up faeces by any caste, not just dalits.

What has really changed for the scavengers in the larger context of a changing India? For the large mass of them in smaller towns and villages, nothing has changed, except that officially they are now given a piece of tin, broom, bucket, and often a tractor to carry the faeces. In larger towns and cities, where the practice of dry latrines has changed and given way to pour-flush toilets, the change is illusory, as the scavengers now continue to clean drains, nalas, septic latrines, sewage pits, and work as municipal sweepers and cleaners. Those recruited by the municipalities and gram panchayats over the past twenty years are not even regular employees; they work as contract labourers for years together on a daily wage.

---

1   Cited in Srivastava, *Manual Scavenging*, 106.
2   N.R. Malkani, "Report of the Committee on Customary Rights to Scavenging," cited in Srivastava, *Manual Scavenging*, 136.
3   Bindeshwar Pathak, in his *Road to Freedom* (Delhi: Motilal Banarsidass, 1991), quotes his own survey among 150 scavengers. All said no, when asked if they liked their profession and whether they wanted their children to continue in it. Of them, 26 percent from Patna had made efforts to change their occupation, but in vain. Fifty-four percent replied that they would change their occupation if they could, even if it meant lesser income.

11
What You Can Do

We encounter manual scavenging only in discussions of caste and untouchability. Scavenging thus appears to be the burden of the dalits, not of the other castes who profit by it. The state profits because of the saved capital it can divert from public sanitation works to other sectors, and other castes gain because they can conveniently forget that cleaning after themselves should be their own job. Since sanitation and inadequate sewage disposal adversely affect the health of largely poor people, it is also an issue of class. If it is entirely the problem of the scavengers, it makes sense that they boycott scavenging work and demolish dry toilets. This implies the absolute need for a vigorous organisation of the scavengers themselves—as pioneered by the SKA in Andhra Pradesh. The petition in the Supreme Court is an effort to prod the state; projecting the issue in the media could possibly prod civil society. The focus of dalit organisations on the issue of manual scavenging is yet lacking, but has the potential to transform the lives of manual scavengers. In an age where mechanisation with harvesters, tractors and poclains has rendered thousands of manual labourers jobless, it is a standing testimony to the lasting virulence of the caste system that public facility cleaning and sewage disposal are still handled by human beings.

Local initiatives

Wherever you live, there is a lot you can do. To start with, you could reflect upon and question the skewed distribution of resources.

Why is it that the major cities (and within them, localities where the rich live such as Jubilee Hills and Banjara Hills in Hyderabad) grab a major portion of funds allocated for infrastructural resources like sanitation? Why is it that our elected representatives and officials concentrate on water supply, but not on sanitation and sewage that adversely affect the health of largely poor people?

If you are in a municipality or gram panchayat, find out if there are community dry latrines and individual dry latrines in your area. The list in Appendix 3 should help you if you are in Andhra Pradesh. Please try to access a similar list in your state using the organisations listed in Appendix 1. You could visit the local colony of people who do the scavenging work and take their help. But make sure you do not patronise them. It helps to gather friends and like-minded people with you. Once you identify the dry toilets, write a letter to the chairperson/commissioner, or sarpanch/president of your local authority giving the details, and asking that they abolish these immediately. It would also help to meet the local revenue officer, revenue divisional officer and collector, as well as the police authorities, to request their help and intervention. You may have to show them the Employment of Manual Scavengers and Construction of Dry Latrines (Prohibition) Act, 1993, (see Appendix 2) and its provisions since many of them may be unaware of it. You will need to reactivate all these agencies and remind them of their constitutional duties. Authorities seldom act on the basis of a single letter. They have to be pressured in multiple ways.

It would also help if you contact the local media, both print and electronic, take them around the dry toilets, and ensure coverage. You could insist that mediapersons elicit the views of the elected representatives on their awareness about the dry toilets in their constituencies, and what they are going to do about it. Letters in newspapers and magazines would help. Elected representatives will be forced to take notice once the matter is made public. Celebrities, prominent academics, writers, poets, musicians, dancers and the notable rich could also be roped in to raise awareness.

Organisations that work on focused issues such as child labour, atrocities on women, education of deprived children, human rights, civil liberties, and animal rights could also mobilised for a campaign against dry latrines and manual scavenging. Besides, there are student organisations and organisations of the Left and Right that could be involved. This is not an issue that concerns manual scavengers alone. It concerns everybody in society. The safai karamcharis do it because they are forced to, but we tolerate and encourage manual scavenging because we are lesser human beings. Any effort we make is for our own redemption.

APPENDIX 1

List of people/organisations you can contact across India to initiate action against dry latrines and manual scavenging

	Name	Organisation	Address	Phone/email
1	Bezwada Wilson	Safai Karmachari Andolan (SKA)	942, Street No. 7 Bakaram, Gandhinagar Hyderabad—500080 **Andhra Pradesh**	040-55258033 ska_hyd@yahoo.co.in
2	N.Paul Diwakar	National Campaign for Dalit Human Rights (NCDHR)	"	93501 83801
3	Deepthi Sukumar	SKA	19, NCC Campus Tambaram Chennai—600 057 **Tamil Nadu**	044-22391147
4	D. Babulal	SKA	M/019, Smith Road Marikuppam KGF, Kolar **Karnataka**	09886852170
5	Y. Moses	SKA	55, Swarna Marg 10th Cross, 3rd Main Hoysalanagar Bangalore **Karnataka**	080-25653324
6	S. Muralidhar	Advocate Supreme Court	283, Supreme Enclave Mayur Vihar Phase 1 **New Delhi**—110091	011-22755116
7	Rani	SKA	34/15, 1st floor East Patel Nagar **New Delhi**—110 008	011-25863166 09818896119 ska_delhi@vsnl.net

Name	Organisation	Address	Phone/email
8 Sohanlal Sarwan	SKA	H.NO. 1159 F/26 Vishal Nagar, Ajmer **Rajasthan**	0145-2692073 0141-2281509
9 Akhil Chandra Misra	Action Aid	A-3 Vivekanandanagar South East Colony Patna, **Bihar**—13	0612-2262027 2272928
10 Barbir Singh	HCPRF	Panipat, **Haryana**	0180-2572480
11 Subhash Desawara	NCDHR	24, New colony Near SDP College Ludhiana—141 008 **Punjab**	09316814245 09888011704 09417003367
12 Basanth Pradhan	Orissa Shramik Adhikar Manch	c/o NSS office PTC, **Orissa**	06764-234223
13 Gurusevak	Jammu Adi Dharma Samaj	Valmiki Colony Gandhinagar **Jammu**	0191-439519
14 Jung Bahadur	Valmiki Welfare Association	Valmiki Mohalla Gandhinagar **Jammu**	0191-2457863 09419184193
15 Jayesh Parmar	Navsarjan	Ahmedabad **Gujarat**	079-55443745 55443746
16 —	Abhiyan	Jan Sahas Dewar—455 001 **Madhya Pradesh**	098264-23634
17 R.H. Haralkar	Safai Kamgar Parivarthan Sangh	E2/13, Sector 48 Nerul, Opp. DAV Public School Navi Mumbai **Maharashtra**	022-27724477
18 Rak Kumar	SKA	Naraina village Panipat district **Haryana**	0180-2572480
19 Pushpa Balmiki	Adharshila	A-22/780 Lavakush Nagar Lucknow—226016 **Uttar Pradesh**	09415142146 09335291289

APPENDIX 2

The Employment of Manual Scavengers and Construction of Dry Latrines (Prohibition) Act, 1993

(No. 46 of 1993)

[5 June 1993]

An Act to provide for the prohibition of employment of manual scavengers as well as construction or continuance of dry latrines and for the regulation of construction and maintenance of water-seal latrines and for matters connected therewith or incidental thereto.

WHEREAS fraternity assuring the dignity of the individual has been enshrined in the Preamble to the Constitution;

AND WHEREAS article 47 of the Constitution, inter alia, provides that the State shall regard raising the standard of living of its people and the improvement of public health as among its primary duties;

AND WHEREAS the dehumanising practice of manual scavenging of human excreta still continues in many parts of the country;

AND WHEREAS the municipal laws by themselves as a measure for conversion of dry latrines into water-seal latrines and prevention of construction of dry latrines are not stringent enough to eliminate this practice;

AND WHEREAS it is necessary to enact a uniform legislation for the whole of India for abolishing manual scavenging by declaring employment of manual scavengers for removal of human excreta an offence and thereby ban the further proliferation of dry latrines in the country;

AND WHEREAS it is desirable for eliminating the dehumanising practice of employment of manual scavengers And for protecting and improving the human environment to make it obligatory to convert dry latrines into water-seal latrines or to construct water-seal latrines in new construction;

AND WHEREAS Parliament has no power to make laws for the States with respect to the matters aforesaid, except as provided in Articles 249 and 250 of the Constitution;

AND WHEREAS in pursuance of clause (1) of Article 252 of the Constitution, resolutions have been passed by all the Houses of the Legislature of the States of Andhra Pradesh, Goa, Karnataka, Maharashtra, Tripura and West Bengal that the matters aforesaid should be regulated in those State by Parliament by law;

Be it enacted by Parliament in the Forty-fourth Year of the Republic of India as follows:

CHAPTER I
PRELIMINARY

1. **Short title, application and commencement**

    (1) This Act may be called the Employment of Manual Scavengers and Construction of Dry Latrines (Prohibition) Act, 1993.

    (2) It applies in the first instance to the whole of the States of Andhra Pradesh, Goa, Karnataka, Maharashtra, Tripura and West Bengal and to all the Union Territories and it shall also apply to such other States which adopt this Act by resolution passed in that behalf under clause (1) of Article 252 of the Constitution.

    (3) It shall come into force in the States of Andhra Pradesh, Goa, Karnataka, Maharashtra, Tripura and West Bengal and in the Union Territories on such date as the Central Government may, by notification, appoint and in any other State which adopts this Act under clause (1) of Article 252 of the Constitution, on the date of such adoption.

2. **Definitions**

    In this Act, unless the context otherwise requires,

    (a) "area", in relation to any provision of this Act, means such area as the State Government may, having regard to the requirements of that provision, specify by notification;

    (b) "building" means a house, out-house stable, latrine, urinal, sheet house, hut, wall (other than a boundary wall) or any other structure whether made of masonry, bricks, wood, mud, metal or other material;

    (c) "dry latrines" means a latrine other than a water-seal latrine;

    (d) "environment" includes water, air and land and the inter-relationship which exist among and between water, air and land and human beings, other living creatures, plants, organisms and property;

    (e) "environmental pollutant" means any solid, liquid or gaseous substance present in such concentration as may be, or tend to be, injurious to environment;

    (f) "environmental pollution" means the presence in the environment of any environmental pollutant;

    (g) "Executive Authority" means an Executive Authority appointed under sub-section (1) Section 5;

(h) "HUDCO" means the Housing and Urban Development Corporation Limited, a Government company registered by that name under the Companies Act, 1956;

(i) "latrine" means a place set apart for defecation together with the structure comprising such place, the receptacle therein for collection of human excreta and the fittings and apparatus, if any, connected therewith;

(j) "manual scavenger" means a person engaged in or employed for manually carrying human excreta and the expression "manual scavenging" shall be construed accordingly;

(k) "notification" means a notification published in the official Gazette;

(l) "prescribed" means prescribed by rules made under this Act;

(m) "State Government", in relation to a Union Territory, means the Administrator thereof appointed under Article 239 of the Constitution;

(n) "water-seal latrine" means a pour-flush latrine, water-flush latrine or a sanitary latrine with a minimum water-seal of 20 millimetres diameter in which human excreta is pushed in or flushed by water.

CHAPTER II
PROHIBITION OF EMPLOYMENT OF MANUAL SCAVENGERS, ETC.

3. Prohibition of employment of manual scavengers, etc.

(1) Subject to sub-Section (2) and the other provisions of this Act, with effect from such date and in such area as the State Government may, by notification, specify in this behalf, no person shall

(a) engage in or employ for or permit to be engaged in or employed for any other person for manually carrying human excreta; or

(b) construct or maintain a dry latrine.

(2) The State Government shall not issue a notification under sub-Section (1) unless

(i) it has, by notification, given not less than ninety days' notice of its intention to do so;

(ii) adequate facilities for the use of water-seal latrines in that area exist; and

(iii) it is necessary or expedient to do so for the protection and improvement of the environment or public health in that area.

4. Power to exempt

The State Government may, by a general or special order published in the Official Gazette, and upon such conditions, if any, as it may think fit to impose, exempt any area, category of buildings or class of persons from any provisions of this Act or from any specified requirement contained in this Act or any rule, order, notification or scheme made thereunder or dispense with the observance of any such requirement in a class or classes of cases, if it is satisfied that compliance with such provisions or such requirement is or ought to be exempted or dispensed with in the circumstances of the case.

CHAPTER III
IMPLEMENTING AUTHORITIES AND SCHEMES

5. Appointment of Executive Authorities and their powers and functions

(1) The State Government may, by order published in the Official Gazette, appoint a District Magistrate or a Sub-divisional Magistrate, as an Executive Authority to exercise jurisdiction within such area as may be specified in the order and confer such powers and impose such duties on him, as may be necessary to ensure that the provisions of this Act are properly carried out and the Executive Authority may specify the officer or officers, subordinate to him, who shall exercise all or any of the powers, and perform all or any of the duties, so conferred or imposed and the local limits within which such powers or duties shall be carried out by the officer or officers so specified.

(2) The Executive Authority appointed under sub-Section (1) and the officer or officers specified under that sub-Section shall, as far as practicable, try to rehabilitate and promote the welfare of the persons who were engaged in or employed for as manual scavengers in any area in respect of which a notification under sub-Section (1) of Section 3 has been issued by securing and protecting their economic interests.

6. Power of State Government to make schemes

(1) The State Government may, by notification, make one or more schemes for regulating conversion of dry latrines into, or construction and maintenance of, water-seal latrines, rehabilitation of the persons who were engaged in or employed for as manual scavengers in any area in respect of which a notification under sub-Section(l) of Section 3 has been issued in gainful employment and administration of such schemes and different schemes may be made in relation to different areas and for different purposes of this Act:

> Provided that no such schemes as involving financial assistance from the HUDCO shall be made without consulting it.

(2) In particular, and without prejudice to the generality of the foregoing power, such schemes may provide for all or any of the following matters, namely:

(a) time-bound phased programme for the conversion of dry latrines into water-seal latrines;

(b) provisions of technical or financial assistance for new or alternate low cost sanitation to local bodies or other agencies;

(c) construction and maintenance of community latrines and regulation of their use on pay and use basis;

(d) construction and maintenance of shared latrines in slum areas or for the benefit of socially and economically backward classes of citizens;

(e) registration of manual scavengers and their rehabilitation;

(f) specification and standards of water-seal latrines;

(g) procedure for conversion of dry latrines into water-seal latrines;

(h) licensing for collection of fees in respect of community latrines or shared latrines.

7. Power of State Government to issue directions

Notwithstanding anything contained in any other law but subject to the other provisions of this Act, the State Government may, in the exercise of its powers and performance of its functions under this Act, issue directions in writing to any person, officer or local or other authority and such person, officer or a local or other authority shall be bound to comply with such directions.

8. Executive authorities, inspectors, officers and other employees of such authorities to be public servants

All Executive Authorities, all officers and other employees of such authorities including the officers authorised under sub-Section (1) of Section 5, all inspectors appointed under sub-Section (1) of Section 9 and all officers and other employees authorised to execute a scheme or order made under this Act, when acting or purporting to act in pursuance of any provisions of this Act or the rules or schemes made or orders or directions issued thereunder, shall be deemed to be public servants within the meaning of Section 21 of the Indian Penal Code (45 of 1860).

9. Appointment of inspectors and their powers of entry and inspection

(1) The State Government may, by notification, appoint such persons as it may think fit to be inspectors for the purposes of this Act, and define the local limits within which they shall exercise their powers under this Act.

(2) Every inspector within the local limits of jurisdiction of an Executive Authority shall be subordinate to such authority.

(3) Subject to any rules made in this behalf by the State Government, an inspector may, within the local limits of his jurisdiction, enter, at all reasonable times, with such assistance as he considers necessary, any place for the purpose of

(a) performing any of the functions of the Executive Authority entrusted to him;

(b) determining whether and if so in what manner, any such functions are to be performed or whether any provisions of this Act or the rules, orders or schemes made thereunder or any notice, directions or authorisation served, made, given or granted under this Act is being or has been complied with;

(c) examining and testing any latrine or for conducting an inspection of any building in which he has reasons to believe that an offence under this Act or the rules, orders or schemes made thereunder has been or is being or is about to be committed and to prevent or mitigate environmental pollution.

10. Power of Executive Authority to prevent environmental pollution in certain cases

(1) On receipt of information with respect to the fact or apprehension of any occurrence of contravention of the provisions of Section 3, whether through intimation by some person or on a report of the inspector or otherwise, the Executive Authority shall, as early as practicable, besides taking any other action under this Act, direct the owner or occupier of the premises to take such remedial measures, as may be necessary, within such reasonable time as may be specified therein and in case the owner or occupier, as the case may be, fails to comply with such directions, cause such remedial measures to be taken as are necessary to prevent or mitigate the environmental pollution at the cost of such owner or occupier of the premises.

(2) The expenses, if any, incurred by the Executive Authority with respect to the remedial measures referred to in sub-Section (1), together with interest at such rate as the State Government may specify from the date when a demand for the expenses is made until it is paid, may be recovered by such authority or agency from the person concerned as arrears of land revenue or of public demand.

11. Duty of HUDCO to extend financial assistance in certain cases

(1) Notwithstanding anything contained in its Memorandum of Association or Articles of Association or schemes for the grant of loans for housing and urban development, it shall be the duty of HUDCO to extend, in suitable cases, financial assistance for the implementation of

such schemes for the construction of water-seal latrines as may be made under Section 6.

(2) The financial assistance referred to in sub-Section (1) may be extended by HUDCO on such terms and conditions (including on easy and concessional rates of interest) and in such manner as it may think fit in each case or class of cases.

12. Power to levy fee

Any order or scheme which the State Government is empowered to make under this Act may notwithstanding the absence of any express provision to that effect, provide for levy of fees in respect of

(a) community latrines constructed under a scheme on pay and use basis; or

(b) shared latrines constructed under a scheme; or

(c) supply of copies or documents of orders or extracts thereof; or

(d) licensing of contractors for construction of water-seal latrines; or

(e) any other purpose or matter fit involving rendering of service by any officer, committee, or authority under this Act or any rule, direction, order or scheme made thereunder:

Provided that the State may, if it considers necessary so to do, in the public interest, by general or special order published in the Official Gazette, grant exemption on such grounds as it deems fit from the payment of any such fee either in part or in full.

13. Constitution of committees

(1) The Central Government may, by notification, constitute

(a) one or more Project Committees for appraising of the schemes for the construction of water-seal latrines in the country;

(b) one or more Monitoring Committees to monitor the progress of such schemes;

(c) such other committees for such purposes of the Act and with such names as the Central Government may deem fit.

(2) The composition of the committees constituted by the Central Government, the powers and functions thereof, the terms and conditions of appointment of the members of such committees and other members connected therewith shall be such as the Central Government may prescribe.

(3) The members of the committee under sub-Section (1) shall be paid such fees and allowances for attending the meetings as may be prescribed.

(4) The State Government may, by notification, constitute

(a) one or more State Co-ordination Committees for co-ordinating and monitoring of the programmes for the construction of water-seal latrines in the State and rehabilitation of the persons who were engaged in or employed for as manual scavengers in any area in respect of which a notification under sub-Section (1) of Section 3 has been issued

(b) such other committees for such purpose of the Act and with such names as the State Government may deem fit.

(5) The composition of the committees constituted by the State Government, the powers and functions thereof, the terms and conditions of the members of such committees and other matters connected therewith shall be such as the State Government may prescribe.

(6) The members of the committees under sub-Section (4) shall be paid such fees and allowances for attending the meetings as may be prescribed.

CHAPTER IV
PENALTIES AND PROCEDURE

14. Penalty for contravention of the provisions of the Act and rules, orders, directions and schemes

Whoever fails to comply with or contravenes any of the provisions of this Act, or the rules or schemes made or orders or directions issued thereunder, shall, in respect of each such failure or contravention be punishable with imprisonment for a term which may extend to one year or with fine, which may extend to two thousand rupees, or with both; and in case the failure or contravention continues, with additional fine which may extend to one hundred rupees for every day during which such failure or contravention continues after the conviction for the first such failure or contravention.

15. Offences by companies

(1) If the person committing an offence under this Act is a company, the company as well as every person in charge of, and responsible to, the company for the conduct of its business at the time of the commission of the offence, shall be deemed to be guilty of the offence and shall be liable to be proceeded against and punished accordingly:

Provided that nothing contained in this sub-Section shall render any such person liable to any punishment, if he proves that the offence was committed without his knowledge or that he had exercised all due diligence to prevent the commission of such offence.

(2) Notwithstanding anything contained in sub-Section (1), where an offence under this Act has been committed by a company and it is proved that the offence has been committed with the consent or contrivance of,

or that the commission of the offence is attributable to any neglect on the part of any director, manager, managing agent or such other officer of the company, such director, manager, managing agent or such other officer shall also be deemed to be guilty of that offence and shall be liable to be proceeded against and punished accordingly.

Explanation

For the purposes of this Section

(a) "company" means any body corporate and includes a firm or other association of individuals; and

(b) "director", in relation to a firm, means a partner in the firm.

16. Offences to be cognisable

Notwithstanding anything contained in the Code of Criminal Procedure, 1973, every offence under this Act shall be cognisable.

17. Provision in relation to jurisdiction

(1) No Court inferior to that of a Metropolitan Magistrate or a Judicial Magistrate of the first class shall try any offence under this Act.

(2) No prosecution for any offence under this Act shall be instituted except by or with the previous sanction of the Executive Authority.

(3) No Court shall take cognisance of any offence under this act except upon a complaint made by a person generally or specially authorised in this behalf by the Executive Authority.

18. Limitation of prosecution

No Court shall take cognisance of an offence punishable under this Act unless the complaint thereof is made within three months from the date on which the alleged commission of the offence came to the knowledge of the complaint.

CHAPTER V
MISCELLANEOUS

19. Information, reports or returns

The Central Government may, in relation to its functions under this Act, from time to time, require any person, officer, State Government or other authority to furnish to it, any prescribed authority or officer any reports, returns, statistics, accounts and other information as may be deemed necessary and such person, officer, State Government or other authority, as the case may be, shall be bound to do so.

20. Protection of action taken in good faith

No suit, prosecution or other legal proceedings shall lie against the

Government or any officer or other employee of the Government or any authority constituted under this Act or executing any scheme made under this Act or any member, officer or other employee of such authority or authorities in respect of anything which is done or intended to be done in good faith in pursuance of this Act or the rules or schemes made, or the orders or directions issued, thereunder.

21. Effect of other laws and agreements inconsistent with the Act

(1) Subject to the provisions of sub-Section (2), the provisions of this Act, the rules, schemes or orders made thereunder shall have effect notwithstanding anything inconsistent therewith contained in any enactment other than this Act, customs tradition, contract, agreement or other instrument.

(2) If any act or omission constitutes an offence punishable under this Act and also under any other Act, then, the offender found guilty of such offence shall be liable to be punished under the other Act and not under this Act.

22. Power of Central Government to make rules

(1) The Central Government may, by notification, make rules to carry out the provisions of this Act.

(2) Without prejudice to the generality of the foregoing power, such rules may provide for all or any of the following matters, namely:

(i) the composition of the Project Committees, Monitoring Committees and other committees constituted by the Central Government under sub-Section (1) of Section 13, the powers and functions thereof, the number of members and their terms and conditions of appointment and other matters connected therewith;

(ii) the fees and allowances to be paid to the members of the committees constituted under sub-Section (1) of Section 13.

(3) Every rule made by the Central Government under this Act shall be laid, as soon as may be after it is made, before each House of Parliament, while it is in session, for a total period of thirty days which may be comprised in one session or in two or more successive sessions, and if, before the expiry of the session immediately following the session or the successive sessions aforesaid, both Houses agree in making any modification in the rule or both Houses agree that the rule should not be made, the rule shall thereafter have effect only in such modified form or be of no effect, as the case may be; so however that any such modification shall be without prejudice to the validity of anything previously done under that rule.

23. Power of State Government to make rules

(1) The State Government may, by notification, make rules, not being a matter for which the rules are or required to be made by the Central Government, for carrying out the provisions of this Act.

(2) Without prejudice to the generality of the foregoing power, such rules may provide for all or any of the following matters, namely:

(i) the composition of the State Co-ordination Committees and other committees constituted by the State Government under sub-Section (4) of Section 13, the powers and functions thereof, the number of members and their terms and conditions of appointment and other matters connected therewith;

(ii) the fees and allowances to be paid to the members of the committees constituted under sub-Section (4) of Section 13;

(iii) any other matter which is required to be, or may be prescribed.

(3) Every rule and every scheme made by the State Government under this Act shall be laid, as soon as may be after it is made, before the State Legislature.

24. Power to remove difficulties

(1) If any difficulty arises in giving effect to the provisions of this Act, the Central Government may, by order published in the Official Gazette, make such provisions, not inconsistent with the provisions of this Act, as may appear to it to be necessary or expedient for the removal of the difficulty:

Provided that no such order shall be made in relation to a State after the expiration of three years from the commencement of this Act in that State.

(2) Every order made under this Section shall, as soon as may be after it is made, be laid before each House of Parliament.

APPENDIX 3

List of community dry latrines in municipalities and gram panchayats in Andhra Pradesh as on 20 August 2001

District	Municipalities	Gram panchayats	Total
Srikakulam	1,019	70	1,089
Vizianagaram	115	43	158
Visakhapatnam	2,040	211	2,251
E.Godavari	1,026	1,222	2,248
W.Godavari	2,535	970	3,505
Krishna	339	828	1,167
Guntur	45	164	209
Prakasam	72	133	205
Nellore	31	33	64
Kurnool	4,323	459	4,782
Cuddapah	2,108	216	2,324
Anantapur	3,896	277	4,173
Chittoor	18	38	56
Warangal	508	22	530
Karimnagar	184	64	248
Adilabad	98	4	102
Rangareddy	–	–	797
Nalgonda	397	38	435
Mehboobnagar	791	95	886
Khammam	–	–	1
Nizamabad	13	6	19
Medak	438	72	510
Hyderabad	–	–	3
Total	21,067	4,695	25,762

The list of individual dry latrines is incomplete. The Andhra Pradesh Scheduled Castes Cooperative Finance Corporation updates the list of CDLS every month. However, the Safai Karmachari Andolan finds that the updating is not authentic. This list, compiled jointly by SKA and APSCCFC in 2001, is incomplete but not false. While it is true that several demolitions and conversions have taken place, the bulk of the toilets remain in place. Even in this data, several areas such as Kurnool town have remained undocumented.

APPENDIX 4
Mohandas Gandhi on Manual Scavenging

The position that I really long for is that of the Bhangi. How sacred is this work of cleanliness! That work can be done only by a Brahmin or by a Bhangi. The Brahmin may do it in his wisdom, the Bhangi in ignorance. I respect, I adore, both of them. If either of the two disappears from Hinduism, Hinduism itself would disappear.

And it is because *seva-dharma* (*seva*-service) is dear to my heart that the Bhangi is dear to me. I may even sit at my meals with a Bhangi on my side, but I do not ask you to align yourselves with them by intercaste dinners and marriages.

— 8 January 1925[1]

א א א

It is simply superfluous for me to say anything about untouchability. I have often and often declared that if I am destined not to gain redemption in this very life, it is my aspiration to be born a Bhangi in my next birth. I believe in *varnashram* and in both *janma* and *karma* (birth in a particular caste and fate fixed by actions in past births) associated with it, but I refuse to believe that a Bhangi is a born sinner. I have, on the contrary, seen countless Bhangis who deserve my veneration and many among Brahmins whom it becomes a very difficult task to adore. I shall be able to render more service to Bhangis by being born a Bhangi and be able in addition to make other communities see the light in this matter, than I ever can to Brahmins or recluses by being born a Brahmin. I wish to serve the Bhangis in numerous ways. But I do not wish to advise them to detest and hate the Brahmin. Hatred, disgust, causes me deep pain. I do wish the uplift of the Bhangis, but do not regard it my duty to teach them to wrest their rights by the way of the West. It is not our *dharma* to gain anything by that method. Whatever is gained by brute-force is not going to last long in this world and I distinctly perceive the advent of that age in the world when it will be impossible to gain anything by means of physical might.

—*Navajivan*, 11 January 1925[2]

ℵ ℵ ℵ

Varnashrama and untouchability

Does untouchability in the case of a cobbler or scavenger attach to birth or to occupation? If it attaches to birth, it is hideous and must be rooted out; if it attaches to occupation it may be a sanitary rule of great importance. It is of universal application. A collier, whilst he is engaged in his work, is practically an untouchable. He, himself, refuses to shake the hand extended to him and says: "I am too dirty." But his work finished, he takes his bath, changes his dress, and very properly mixes with the highest in the land. Immediately, therefore, we remove the taint of birth, i.e. the idea of superiority and inferiority attaching to birth, we purify *Varnashrama*. The scavenger's children may remain scavengers without being or feeling degraded, and they will be no more considered untouchables than *Brahmins*. The fault does not, therefore, lie in recognizing the Law of Heredity and transmission of qualities from generation to generation, but it lies with the faulty conception of inequality.

Varnashrama, in my opinion, was not conceived in any narrow spirit. On the contrary, it gave the labourer, the *Shudra*, the same status as the thinker, the *Brahmin*. It provided for the accentuation of merit and elimination of demerit, and it transferred human ambition from the general worldly sphere to the permanent and the spiritual. The aim of the *Brahmin* and the *Shudra* was common—*Moksha*, or self-realization—not realization of fame, riches and power. Later on, this lofty conception of *Varnashrama* became degraded and came to be identified with mere empty ceremonial and assumption of superiority by some and imposition of degradation upon others. This admission is not a demonstration of the weakness of *Varnashrama* but of human nature which, if it has a tendency under certain circumstances to rise to the highest point, has also a tendency under certain other circumstances to go down to the lowest. What the reformer seeks to do is to end the curse of untouchability and to restore *Varnashrama* to its proper place. Whether *Varnashrama* thus transmuted will survive the reform or not, remains to be seen. It will surely depend upon the new *Brahmin* class that is imperceptibly coming into being, namely, those who are dedicating themselves, body, soul and mind, to service of Hinduism and the country. If they have nothing of worldly ambition, it will be well with Hinduism; if they have, Hinduism, like any other ism, coming into the hands of ambitious men, will perish. But I have an immutable faith in the capacity of Hinduism to purge itself of all impurities from time to time. I do not think that that capacity is now exhausted.

—*Young India*, 13 August 1925[3]

א א א

The iniquities we, caste-Hindus, have heaped upon you are so many and so horrible, that enough amends cannot be made even if we scraped our own skins and presented you with shoes made from them. I am a non-Brahmin by birth and became a sweeper by action. It is no calamity to be a sweeper. One can become a Bhangi (sweeper) in two ways. Somebody may call me a Bhangi by way of an abuse— as if a sweeper is a burden to society, though he does the very useful work of cleaning latrines and sweeping streets. Or one may call that man a Bhangi whose service of the people reaches its acme. The Bhangi's service is like that of our mothers, but we never call them untouchables. Far from it, the mother is revered as a Goddess worth remembering during our morning prayers. The Bhangi therefore is a true servant of society—with the only difference that he works for earning his bread, while the mother does it in a beneficent spirit. The mother serves the child with love and she gets love in return.

But salary is the return the sweeper gets for his service. Just as we cannot live without mothers, so can we not live without sweepers. That means that by their work they do only their duty to society. Let those who are sweepers among you here know that I can beat the best of them in the excellence of his cleaning work.

To the caste-Hindus I point out only one thing as regards untouchability. I rebuke them, blame them, for observing untouchability which I call a dark spot on Hinduism. As I told you, when I approach the caste-Hindu public I tell it that untouchability is a heinous sin.

But to untouchables themselves I say another thing. You eat putrid flesh, become drunkards, commit adultery and keep yourselves dirty. There is no one present here to bear witness to the strength with which the objectors emphasise these things. Do away with these serious defects. Perhaps nowhere in the world are as many putrid-flesh-eaters as in India. Give up beef, liquor and adultery. An adulterer is just like a beast. But you will protest: 'Do not other people commit the same sins?' I say let them, but I ask you not to do so.

—13 February 1927[4]

א א א

Most honourable occupation

You should know that I am a scavenger myself by choice; and you must take me literally when I tell you that I have cleaned hundreds of *cheris* in my life. Everyone in the *Ashram* which I was conducting—and there were women also in the *Ashram*—had to do this work every day. I call scavenging as one of the most honourable occupations to which mankind is called. I don't consider it an unclean occupation by any means. That you have to handle dirt is true. But that every mother is doing and has to do. But nobody says a mother's occupation is unclean. And yet the scavenger's occupation is considered an unclean occupation. Therefore, I say that those who call themselves caste Hindus commit a sin when they consider themselves higher than Harijans. I am going up and down the country to convince *Savarna* Hindus that it is a sin to consider themselves superior to or higher than anyone else. But I am trying also to tell fellow-scavengers that, while we may handle dirt, we must be clean ourselves both inwardly and outwardly. After we have done the cleansing, we must cleanse ourselves and put on clean clothes. I know many scavengers eat carrion and beef. Those who are doing this must abstain. Many of them are given to the evil habit of drink. Drink is a bad, filthy, unclean, degrading habit. A man who drinks intoxicating liquor forgets the distinction between wife, mother and sister. I would beseech you to give up all evil habits, and you will at once find that you are accepted as honourable members of society without any stain on you.

—*Harijan*, 19 January 1934[5]

ॐ ॐ ॐ

The Ideal Bhangi

The ideal Bhangi of my conception would be a Brahmin par excellence, possibly even excel him. It is possible to envisage the existence of a Bhangi without a Brahmin. But without the former the latter could not be. It is the Bhangi who enables society to live. A Bhangi does for society what a mother does for her baby. A mother washes her baby of the dirt and insures his health. Even so the Bhangi protects and safeguards the health of the entire community by maintaining sanitation for it. The Brahmin's duty is to look after the sanitation of the soul, the Bhangi's that of the body of society. But there is a difference in practice; the Brahmin generally does not live up to his duty, the Bhangi does, willy-nilly no doubt. Society is sustained by several services. The Bhangi constitutes the foundation of all services.

And yet our woebegone Indian society has branded the Bhangi as a social pariah, set him down at the bottom of the scale, held him fit only to receive kicks and abuse, a creature who must subsist on the leavings of the caste people and dwell on the dung-heap. He is without a friend, his very name has become a term of reproach. This is shocking. It is perhaps useless to seek the why and wherefore of it. I certainly am unaware of the origin of the inhuman conduct, but I know this much that by looking down upon the Bhangi, we Hindus, have deserved the contempt of the whole world. Our villages have today become seats of dirt and insanitation and the villagers come to an early and untimely death. If only we had given due recognition to the status of the Bhangi as equal to that of a Brahmin as in fact and justice he deserves, our villages today no less than their inhabitants would have looked a picture of cleanliness and order. We would have to a large extent been free from the ravages of a host of diseases which directly spring from our uncleanliness and lack of sanitary habits. I therefore make bold to state without any manner of hesitation or doubt that not till the invidious distinction between the Brahmin and the Bhangi is removed will our society enjoy health, prosperity and peace, and be happy.

What qualities should such an honoured servant of society exemplify in his person? In my opinion an ideal Bhangi should have a thorough knowledge of the principles of sanitation. He should know how a right kind of latrine is constructed and the correct way of cleaning it. He should know how to overcome and destroy the odour of excreta and the various disinfectants to render them innocuous. He should likewise know the process of converting night-soil and urine into manure.

But that is not all. My ideal Bhangi would know the quality of night-soil and urine. He would keep a close watch on these and give a timely warning to the individual concerned. Thus he will give a timely notice of the results of his examination of the excreta. That presupposes a scientific knowledge of the requirements of his profession. He would likewise be an authority on the subject of disposal of night-soil in small villages as well as big cities and his advice and guidance in the matter would be sought for and freely given to society. It goes without saying that he would have the usual learning necessary for reaching the standard here laid down for his profession. Such an ideal Bhangi, while deriving his livelihood from his occupation, would approach it only as a sacred duty. In other words, he would not dream of amassing wealth out of it. He would consider himself responsible for the proper removal and disposal of all the dirt and night-soil within the area which he serves and regard the maintenance of healthy and sanitary condition within the same as the summum bonum of his existence.

—*Harijan*, 28 November 1936[6]

ℵ ℵ ℵ

Sweepers' strike

There are certain matters in which strikes would be wrong. Sweepers' grievances come in this category. My opinion against sweepers' strikes dates back to about 1897 when I was in Durban. A general strike was mooted there, and the question arose as to whether scavengers should join in it. My vote was registered against the proposal. Just as man cannot live without air, so too he cannot exist for long if his home and surroundings are not clean. One or other epidemic is bound to break out, especially when modern drainage is put out of action.... A *Bhangi* may not give up his work even for a day. And there are many other ways open to him for securing justice.

—*Harijan*, 21 April 1946[7]

ℵ ℵ ℵ

Q. What is the poor sweeper to do when everything else fails? Is the *Bhangi* to continue his service on starvation wages, living in dirt and squalor?

A. I claim that in such cases the proper remedy is not a strike, but a notice to the public in general and the employing corporation in particular that the *Bhangis* must give up the sweeping service which consigns those reserved for that service to a life of starvation and all it means. There is a wide distinction between a strike and an entire discontinuation (not suspension) of service. A strike is a temporary measure in expectation of relief. Discontinuance is giving up of a particular job because there is no expectation of relief. Proper discontinuance presupposes fair notice on the one hand, and prospect of better wages and freedom from squalor and dirt on the other. This will wake up society from its disgraceful slumber, resulting in a proper scavenging of the overgrowth that has smothered public conscience. At a stroke, the *Bhangis* will raise scavenging to a fine art and give it the status it should have had long ago.

—*Harijan*, 23 June 1946[8]

א א א

Someone asked Gandhiji whether the adoption of the flush system was not the means of eradicating untouchability and whether he would oppose it on account of his dislike of machinery. He replied:

"Where there is ample supply of water and modern sanitation can be introduced without any hardship on the poor, I have no objection to it. My opposition to machinery is much misunderstood. I am not opposed to machinery as such. I am opposed to machinery which displaces labour and leaves it idle. Whether the flush system will remove the curse of untouchability is open to grave doubt. This latter has to go from our hearts. It will not disappear through such means as has been suggested. Not until we all become *bhangis* and realize the dignity of the labour of scavenging and latrine-cleaning will untouchability really be exorcized."

—*Harijan*, 15 September 1946[9]

א א א

You, friends, have not seen the real India and you are not meeting in conference in the midst of real India. Delhi, Bombay, Madras, Calcutta, Lahore—all these are big cities and are, therefore, influenced by the West. If you really want to see India at its best, you have to find it in the humble *Bhangi* homes of the villages. There are 7,00,000 of such villages and 38 crores of people inhabit them.

If some of you see the villages, you will not be fascinated by the sight. You will have to scratch below the dung-heap. I do not pretend to say that they were ever places of paradise. Today, they are really dung-heaps. They were not like that before. What I speak is not from history, but from what I have seen myself. I have travelled from one end of India to the other, and I have seen the miserable specimens of humanity with lustreless eyes. They are India. In these humble cottages, in the midst of these dung-heaps, are to be found the humble *Bhangis* in whom you find the concentrated essence of wisdom.

—*Harijan*, 20 April 1947[10]

1. From the speech made by Gandhi on his election as president of the Kathiawar (Saurashtra) Political Conference held at Bhavanagar on 8 January 1925. From *Day-to-Day with Gandhi*, Vol. V. By Mahadev H. Desai, p. 136. Accessed at http://web.mahatma.org.in/books/showbook.jsp?link=og&book=og0012&id=136&lang=en&file=5842&cat=books
2. From *Day-to-Day with Gandhi*, Vol. V. By Mahadev H. Desai, p. 334. Accessed at http://web.mahatma.org.in/books/showbook.jsp?link=og&book=og0012&id=334&lang=en&file=6040&cat=book
3. From *My Varnasharama Dharma* in *Gandhi for 21st Century*, Vol. XII, Ed. Anand T. Hingorani, p. 28. Accessed at http://web.mahatma.org.in/books/showbook.jsp?id=42&link=bg&book=bg0017&lang=en&cat=books
4. From *Day-to-Day with Gandhi*, Vol. IX. By Mahadev H. Desai, p. 182. Accessed at http://web.mahatma.org.in/books/showbook.jsp?id=182&link=og&book=og0025&lang=en&cat=books
5. From *Gandhi for 21st Century*, Vol. XI, Ed. Anand T. Hingorani, p. 76. Accessed at http://web.mahatma.org.in/books/showbook.jsp?id=135&link=bg&book=bg0018&lang=en&cat=books
6. Reproduced in *Collected Works of Mahatma Gandhi*, Vol. LXIV, pp. 86-88. Accessed at http://www.gandhiserve.org/cwmg/VOL070. PDF
7. From *Capital and Labour*, in *Gandhi for 21st Century*, Ed. Anand T. Hingorani, p. 86. Accessed at http://web.mahatma.org.in/books/showbook.jsp?link=bg&book=bg0058&id=101&lang=en&file=9251&cat=books
8. From *Capital and Labour*, in *Gandhi for 21st Century*, Ed. Anand T. Hingorani, p. 87. Accessed at http://web.mahatma.org.in/books/showbook.jsp?link=bg&book=bg0058&id=102&lang=en&file=9252&cat=books

9 From *A Gandhi Anthology*, Book II Compiled by Valji Govindji Desai, p. 58. Accessed at http://www.mahatma.org.in/books/showbook.jsp?link=bg&book=bg0014&id=62&lang=en&file=1354&cat=books

10 From an address at the concluding session of the Inter-Asian Relations Conference, Delhi, 2 April 1947, reported in *Harijan*. Accessed at http://web.mahatma.org.in/books/showbook.jsp?link=bg&book=bg0060&id=138&lang=en&file=9519&cat=books

APPENDIX 5
B.R. Ambedkar on Manual Scavenging

Gandhism: The Doom of the Untouchables[Φ]

Gandhism is a paradox. It stands for freedom from foreign domination, which means the destruction of the existing political structure of the country. At the same time it seeks to maintain intact a social structure which permits the domination of one class by another on a hereditary basis which means a perpetual domination of one class by another. What is the explanation of this paradox? Is it a part of a strategy by Mr. Gandhi to win the whole-hearted support of the Hindus, orthodox and unorthodox, to the campaign of Swaraj? If it is the latter, can Gandhism be regarded as honest and sincere? Be that as it may, there are two features of Gandhism which are revealing but to which unfortunately no attention has so far been paid. Whether they will make Gandhism more acceptable than Marxism is another matter. But as they do help to distinguish Gandhism from Marxism, it may be well to refer to them.

The first special feature of Gandhism is that its philosophy helps those who have to keep what they have and to prevent those who have not from getting what they have a right to get. No one who examines the Gandhian attitude to strikes, the Gandhian reverence for Caste and the Gandhian doctrine of Trusteeship by the rich for the benefit of the poor can deny that this is the upshot of Gandhism.

Φ Excerpted from *What Congress and Gandhi have done to the Untouchables*, in *Dr. Babasaheb Ambedkar: Writings and Speeches*, Vol. 9 (Mumbai: Government of Maharashtra, 1990), 290–93.

Whether this is the calculated result of a deliberate design or whether it is a matter of accident may be open to argument. But the fact remains that Gandhism is the philosophy of the well-to-do and the leisure class.

The second special feature of Gandhism is to delude people into accepting their misfortunes by presenting them as the best of good fortunes. One or two illustrations will suffice to bring out the truth of this statement.

The Hindu sacred law penalized the Shudras (Hindus of the fourth class) from acquiring wealth. It is a law of enforced poverty unknown in any other part of the world. What does Gandhism do? It does not lift the ban. It blesses the Shudra for his moral courage to give up property! It is well worth quoting Mr. Gandhi's own words. Here they are[1]:

> "The Shudra who only serves (the higher caste) as a matter of religious duty, and who will never own any property, who indeed has not even the ambition to own anything, is deserving of thousand obeisance. The very Gods will shower down flowers on him."

Another illustration in support is the attitude of Gandhism towards the scavenger. The sacred law of the Hindus lays down that a scavenger's progeny shall live by scavenging. Under Hinduism scavenging was not a matter of choice, it was a matter of forced labour. What does Gandhism do? It seeks to perpetuate this system by praising scavenging as the noblest service to society!! Let me quote Mr. Gandhi: As President of a Conference of the Untouchables, Mr. Gandhi said[2]:

> "I do not want to attain Moksha. I do not want to be reborn. But if I have to be reborn, I should be born an untouchable, so that I may share their sorrows, sufferings and the affronts levelled at them, in order that I may endeavour to free myself and them from that miserable condition. I, therefore prayed that if I should be born again, I should do so not as a Brahmin, Kshatriya, Vaishya, or Shudra, but as an Atishudra.

"I love scavenging. In my Ashram, an eighteen year old Brahmin lad is doing the scavenger's work in order to teach the Ashram cleanliness. The lad is no reformer. He was born and bred in orthodoxy. But he felt that his accomplishments were incomplete until he had become also a perfect sweeper, and that if he wanted the Ashram sweeper to do his work well, he must do it himself and set an example.

"You should realise that you are cleaning Hindu Society."

Can there be a worse example of false propaganda than this attempt of Gandhism to perpetuate evils which have been deliberately imposed by one class over another? If Gandhism preached the rule of poverty for all and not merely for the Shudra, the worst that could be said about it is that it is a mistaken idea. But why preach it as good for one class only? Why appeal to the worst of human failings, namely, pride and vanity in order to make him voluntarily accept what on a rational basis he would resent as a cruel discrimination against him? What is the use of telling the scavenger that even a Brahmin is prepared to do scavenging when it is clear that according to Hindu Shastras and Hindu notions even if a Brahmin did scavenging he would never be subject to the disabilities of one who is a born scavenger? For in India a man is not a scavenger because of his work. He is a scavenger because of his birth irrespective of the question whether he does scavenging or not. If Gandhism preached that scavenging is a noble profession with the object of inducing those who refuse to engage in it, one could understand it. But why appeal to the scavenger's pride and vanity in order to induce him and him only to keep on to scavenging[3] by telling him that scavenging is a noble profession and that he need not be ashamed of it? To preach that poverty is good for the Shudra and for none else, to preach that scavenging is good for the Untouchables and for none else and to make them accept these onerous impositions as voluntary purposes of life, by appeal to their failings is an outrage and a cruel joke on the helpless classes which none but Mr. Gandhi can perpetuate with equanimity and impunity.

In this connection one is reminded of the words of Voltaire who in repudiation of an 'ism' very much like Gandhism said: "Oh! mockery to say to people that the suffering of some brings joy to others and works good to the whole. What solace is it to a dying man to know that from his decaying body a thousand worms will come into life?"

Criticism apart, this is the technique of Gandhism, to make wrongs done appear to the very victim as though they were his privileges. If there is an 'ism' which has made full use of religion as an opium to lull the people into false beliefs and false security, it is Gandhism. Following Shakespeare one can well say: Plausibility! Ingenuity! Thy name is Gandhism.

א א א

The Revolt of the Untouchables[Φ]

If the Untouchables skin and carry the dead animals of the Hindus, it is because the Untouchables have no choice. They are forced to do it. They would be penalised if they refused to do it. The penalty is legal. In some provinces the refusal to do this dirty work is a breach of contract. In other provinces it is a criminal offence involving fines. In provinces like Bombay the Untouchables are village servants. In their capacity as village servants they have to serve the Government as well as the Hindu public. In return for this service they are given lands which they cultivate and on the produce of which they maintain themselves. One of the duties of the Untouchables is to skin and carry the dead animals of the Hindus in the villages. If the Untouchables refuse to perform these duties to the Hindu public, the land which they live on is liable to be confiscated. They have to choose between doing the dirty work or facing starvation.

In Provinces like the United Provinces, refusal to do scavenging by sweepers is made an offence. The United Provinces Municipalities

---

Φ Excerpted from *Essays on Untouchables and Untouchability: Political* in *Dr. Babasaheb Ambedkar: Writings and Speeches*, Vol. 5 (Mumbai: Government of Maharashtra, 1989), 256–58.

Act II of 1916 contains the following provisions:

> Section 201(1).— "Should a sweeper who has a customary right to do the house-scavenging of a house or building (hereinafter called the customary sweeper) fail to perform such scavenging in a proper way, the occupier of the house or building or the board may complain to a Magistrate."
>
> (2) "The Magistrate receiving such complaint shall hold an inquiry and should it appear to him that the customary sweeper has failed to perform the house-scavenging of the house or building in a proper way or at a reasonable intervals, he may impose upon such a sweeper a fine which may extend to ten rupees, and upon a second or any later conviction in regard to the same house or building, may also direct, the right of the customary sweeper to do the house-scavenging of the house or building to be forfeited and thereupon such right shall be forfeited."

Exactly similar provision is to be found in Section 165 of the Punjab Municipalities Act of 1911. The Punjab Act is an advance over the U.P. Act, in as much as it provides for punishment of a sweeper who is not a customary sweeper but a contract-sweeper. The Punjab Act adds:

> "(3) Should any sweeper (other than a customary sweeper), who is under a contract to do house-scavenging of a house or a building, discontinue to do such house-scavenging without fourteen days' notice to his employer or without reasonable cause, he shall on conviction be punishable with a fine which may extend to Rs. ten."
>
> "227. Every order of forfeiture under Section 165 shall be subject to an appeal to the next superior court, but shall not be otherwise open to appeal."

People may be shocked to read that there exists legal provision which sanctions forced labour. Beyond doubt, this is slavery. The difference between slavery and free labour lies in this. Under slavery a breach of contract of service is an offence which is punishable with fine or imprisonment. Under free labour a breach of contract of service is only a civil wrong for which the labourer is liable only for damages. Judged in the light of this criterion, scavenging is a legal obligation imposed upon the Untouchables which they cannot escape.

Given these conditions, how can the Untouchables be accused of doing this dirty work voluntarily? The question whether the Untouchables can be accused of having invited the curse of untouchability upon themselves for doing the dirty work of the Hindus is really beside the point. What is important to note is that the Conference of the Untouchables which met in Mahad resolved that no Untouchable shall skin the dead animals of the Hindus, shall carry it or eat the carrion. The object of these resolutions was two-fold. The one object was to foster among the Untouchables self-respect and self-esteem. This was a minor object. The major object was to strike a blow at the Hindu Social Order. The Hindu Social Order is based upon a division of labour which reserves for the Hindus clean and respectable jobs and assigns to the Untouchables dirty and mean jobs and thereby clothes the Hindus with dignity and heaps ignominy upon the Untouchables. The resolution was a revolt against this part of the Hindu Social Order. It aimed at making the Hindus do their dirty jobs themselves.

This is a brief summary of the history of the revolt of the Untouchables against the established order of the Hindus. It originated in Bombay. But it has spread to all parts of India.

א א א

Occupational Origin of Untouchability[Φ]

We may now turn to the occupational theory of the origin of Untouchability. According to Mr. Rice, the origin of Untouchability

---

[Φ] Excerpted from *The Untouchables: Who were they and why they became Untouchables?* in *Dr. Babasaheb Ambedkar: Writings and Speeches*, Vol. 7 (Mumbai: Government of Maharashtra, 1990), 305–07.

is to be found in the unclean and filthy occupations of the Untouchables. The theory is a very plausible one. But there are certain difficulties in the way of its being accepted as a true explanation of the origin of Untouchability. The filthy and unclean occupations which the Untouchables perform are common to all human societies. In every human society there are people who perform these occupations. Why were such people not treated as Untouchables in other parts of the world? The second question is: Did the Dravidians have a nausea against such callings or against persons engaged in them? On this point, there is no evidence. But we have evidence about the Aryans. That evidence shows that the Aryans were like other people and their notions of purity and impurity did not fundamentally differ from those of other ancient people. One has only to consider the following texts from Narada Smriti to show that the Aryans did not at all mind engaging themselves in filthy occupations. In Chapter V Narada is dealing with the subject matter of breach of contract of service. In this Chapter, there occur the following verses:

> 1. The sages have distinguished five sorts of attendants according to law. Among these are four sorts of labourers; the slaves (are the fifth category of which there are) fifteen species.
>
> 2. A student, an apprentice, a hired servant, and fourthly an official.
>
> 3. The sages have declared that the state of dependence is common to all these but their respective position and income depends on their particular caste and occupations.
>
> 4. Know that there are two sorts of occupations; pure work and impure work; *impure work is that done by the slaves.* Pure work is that done by labourers.
>
> 5. *Sweeping the gateway, the privy, the road and the place for rubbish; shampooing the secret parts of the body; gathering and putting away the leaving of food, ordure and urine.*

> 6. *And lastly, rubbing the master's limbs when desired; this should be regarded as impure work. All other work besides this is pure.*
>
> 25. Thus have the four classses of servants doing pure work been enumerated. All the others who do dirty work are slaves, of whom there are fifteen kinds.[4]

It is clear that impure work was done by the slaves and that the impure work included scavenging. The question that arises is: Who were these slaves? Were they Aryans or non-Aryans? That slavery existed among the Aryans admits of no doubt. An Aryan could be a slave of an Aryan. No matter to what Varna an Aryan belonged he could be a slave. A Kshatriya could be a slave. So could a Vaishya. Even a Brahmin was not immune from the law of slavery. It is when *Chaturvarna* came to be recognized as a law of the land that a change was made in the system of slavery. What this change was can be seen from the following extract from the Narada Smriti:

> "39. In the inverse order of the (four) castes slavery is not ordained, except where a man violated the duties peculiar to his caste. Slavery (in that respect) is analogous to the condition of a wife."

Yajnavalkya also says that:

> "183(2) Slavery is in the descending order of the Varnas and not in the ascending order."

This is explained by Vijnaneswara in his Mitakshara, a commentary on Yajnavalkya Smriti in the following terms:

> "Of the Varna such as the Brahmin and the rest, a state of slavery shall exist in the descending order (Anulomeyna). Thus, of a Brahmin, a Kshatriya, and the rest may become a slave; of a Kshatriya, the Vaishya and the Shudra; and of a Vaishya, a Shudra; this state of slavery shall operate in the descending order."

The change was a mere reorganisation of slavery and the basis of the principles of graded inequality which is the soul of Chaturvarna.

To put it in a concrete form, the new law declared that a Brahmin could have a Brahmin, Kshatriya, Vaishya and a Shudra as his slave. A Kshatriya could have Kshatriya, a Vaishya and a Shudra as his slave. A Vaishya could have a Vaishya and a Shudra as his slave. A Shudra could have a Shudra only. With all this, the law of slavery remained and all Aryans whether they were Brahmins, Kshatriyas, Vaishyas or Shudras if they become slaves were subject to it.

Having regard to the duties prescribed for the slaves, this change in the law of slavery does not matter at all. It still means that a Brahmin if he was a slave, a Kshatriya if he was a slave, a Vaishya if he was a slave, did the work of a scavenger. Only a Brahmin would not do scavenging in the house of a Kshatriya, Vaishya or a Shudra. But he would do scavenging in the house of a Brahmin. Similarly, a Kshatriya would do scavenging in the house of a Brahmin and the Kshatriya. Only he would not do in the house of a Vaishya or Shudra and a Vaishya would do scavenging in the house of a Brahmin, Kshatriya and Vaishya. Only he would not do it in the house of a Shudra. It is, therefore, obvious that the Brahmins, Kshatriyas and Vaishyas who are admittedly the Aryans did the work of scavengers which is the filthiest of filthy occupations. If scavenging was not loathsome to an Aryan how can it be said that engaging in filthy occupations was the cause of Untouchability. The theory of filthy occupation as an explanation of Untouchability is, therefore, not tenable.

א א א

Conversion of Sunita, the Sweeper[Φ]

1. There lived in Rajagraha a scavenger by name Sunita. He earned his living as a road sweeper, sweeping away the rubbish thrown by the householders on the roadside. His was a low and hereditary occupation.

Φ Excerpted from *Buddha and His Dhamma* in *Dr. Babasaheb Ambedkar: Writings and Speeches*, Vol. 11 (Mumbai: Government of Maharashtra, 1990), 185–86.

2. One day in the early hours of the dawn the Blessed One rose, dressed himself and walked into Rajagraha for alms followed by a large number of Bhikkus.

3. Now Sunita was cleaning the street, collecting scraps, rubbish, and so on into heaps and filling therewith the basket which he carried on a yoke.

4. And when he saw the Master and his train approaching, his heart was filled with joy and awe.

5. Finding no place to hide in on the road, he placed his yoke in a bend in the wall and stood as if stuck to the wall, saluting the Lord with clasped hands.

6. Then the Lord when he had come near, spoke to him in voice divinely sweet, saying: "Sunita! What to you is this wretched mode of living? Can you endure to leave home and come into the Order?"

7. And Sunita, experiencing the rapture of one who has been sprinkled with Ambrosia, said: "If even such as the Exalted One may in this life take Orders, why should I not? May the Exalted One suffer me to come forth."

8. Then the Master said: "Come Bhikku!" And Sunita by that word received sanction and ordination and was invested with bowl and robes.

9. The Master leading him to the Vihar taught him the Dhamma and the Discipline and said, "By the discipline of holy life, restraint and mastery of self, a man becomes holy."

10. When asked how Sunita became so great, the Buddha said, "As on a rubbish-heap on highway cast a lily may grow, fragrant and sweet, so among rubbish-creatures, worldlings blind by insight shines the very Buddha's child."

---

1   Quoted from *Varna Vyavastha*, p. 51

2 *Young India*, 27th April 1921.

3 Some of the Provinces of India have laws which make refusal by a scavenger to do scavenging a crime for which be can be tried and punished by a criminal court.

4 The fifteen classes of slaves are defined by the Narada Smriti in the following verses:

V. 26. One born at (his master's) house; one purchased one received (by gift); one obtained by inheritance; one maintained during a general famine; one pledged by his rightful owner.

V. 27. One released from heavy debt; one made captive in fight; one won through a wager; one who has come forward declaring 'I am thine'. An apostate from asceticism; one enslaved for a stipulated period,

V. 28. One who has become slave in order to get a maintenance; one enslaved on account of his connection with a female slave; and one self-sold. These are 15 classes of slaves as declared by law.

Select Bibliography

Ambedkar, B.R. *The Untouchables: Who were they and why they became Untouchables?* In Vol. 7 of *Dr. Babasaheb Ambedkar: Writings and Speeches.* Mumbai: Government of Maharashtra, 1990.

——*What Congress and Gandhi have done to the Untouchables.* In Vol. 9. of *Dr. Babasaheb Ambedkar: Writings and Speeches.* Mumbai: Government of Maharashtra, 1990.

AP Mission for Eradication of Manual Scavenging. *Report of the AP Mission for Eradication of Manual Scavenging.* Hyderabad: 2001.

Chaplin, Susan E. "Cities, sewers and poverty: India's politics of sanitation," *Environment and Urbanization,* Vol. 11, No. 1 (April 1999): 145–158.

Feachem, R.G., D.J. Bradley, H. Garelick and D.D. Mara. *Sanitation and Disease: Health Aspects of Excreta and Wastewater Management.* Chicester: John Wiley, 1983.

Joshi, Deepa. "Gender, Urban Sanitation and Livelihoods." *Forthcoming.* Southampton: University of Southampton Press.

Kumar, Prasanna. "Shame." *Deccan Herald,* 15 April 1994.

Kundu, A. *In The Name of the Urban Poor: Access to Basic Amenities.* New Delhi: Sage, 1993.

Malkani, N.R. *Report of the Committee on Customary Rights to Scavenging.* Delhi: Ministry of Home Affairs, 1965.

Molley, L.S.S.O. *Indian Caste Customs.* Delhi: Vikas, 1974.

Pathak, Bindeshwar. *Road to Freedom.* Delhi: Motilal Banarsidass, 1991.

Prashad, Vijay. *Untouchable Freedom: A Social History of a Dalit Community*. New Delhi: Oxford University Press, 2000.

Shyamlal, *The Bhangi: A Sweeper Caste*. Bombay: Popular Prakashan, 1992.

Srinivas, Suvvada. "Coping with Degrading Work: A study of Methars in Hyderabad City." Ph.D. diss., University of Hyderabad, 2003.

Srivastava, B.N., *Manual Scavenging in India: A Disgrace to the Country*. New Delhi: Concept Publishing, 1977.

Thekaekara, Mari Marcel. *Endless Filth: The Saga of the Bhangis*. Bangalore: Books for Change, 2003.

Verma, Gita Dewan. *Slumming India: A Chronicle of Slums and their Saviours*. New Delhi: Penguin, 2002.

Photographs of Public dry latrines

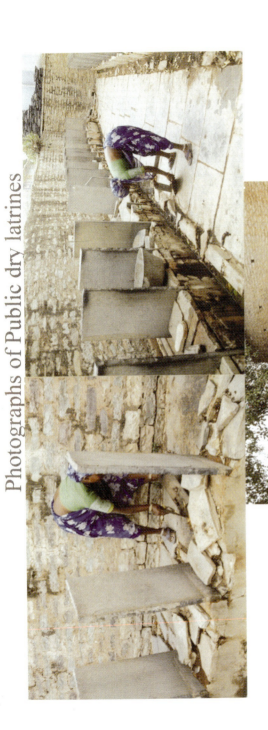

Andhra Pradesh Scheduled Castes Coop Finance Corporation
AP mission on prohibition of manual scavenging
Particulars of Public dry latrines

1. District: Kurnool
2. Municipality / Major Panchayat: Bethamcherla Panchayat
3. Street: Ragimanpeta
4. Landmark: Ragimanpeta, Behind the church
5. No. of seats: Plain area
6. No. of users (average per day): 2 | 6 | 0
7. Scavenger Name: Meramma
8. Municipal Employee / Private: Private Employee, Rs.1500/- per month
9. Availability of water for flushing: No
10. Whether one minute long video clipping is enclosed: Yes

Signature of NGO representative
Date :

Signature of the staff member
District SC society
Date :

Signature of the Executive Director
Date :

Photographs of Public dry latrines

Andhra Pradesh Scheduled Castes Coop Finance Corporation
AP mission on prohibition of manual scavenging
Particulars of Public dry latrines

1. District: Kurnool
2. Municipality / Major Panchayat: Dhone Panchayat
3. Street: H.No.24-91-44, Mastan Doddi, Kondapeta
4. Landmark: Near Dharmavaram Road, Opp:U.P.P.School
5. No. of seats: 2 | 4
6. No. of users (average per day): 4 | 7 | 5
7. Scavenger Name: K.Mariyamma
8. Municipal Employee / Private: Regular Employee – Rs.4030/- per month
9. Availability of water for flushing: No
10. Whether one minute long video clipping is enclosed: Yes

Signature of NGO representative
Date :

Signature of the staff member District SC society
Date :

Signature of the Executive Director
Date :